CW01...

Prehistoric
SKYE

Ian Donaldson-Blyth

Thistle*Press*

Quality guides to Scotland

© Ian Donaldson-Blyth 1995

Cover photograph
Dun Beag (Broch); Central Region
© Ian Donaldson-Blyth, 1995

ISBN   0 9520950 2 5

British Library Cataloguing-in-Publication Data.
A catalogue record for this book is available from the British Library.

Published by
Thistle*Press*,
Insch, Aberdeenshire,
AB52 6JR, Scotland.

THE AUTHOR

Although he was born in London, Ian Donaldson-Blyth's interest in Scotland dates from a very early age, when it was kindled by his grandmother's stories about her family's days in Skye and the Highlands. He served as an aircrew officer in the Royal Air Force from leaving school until he retired as a Wing Commander in 1990, during which time he was stationed in the north of Scotland for several years, and first visited Skye. Since that visit, he has regularly and frequently returned to the Island over the last thirty years.

He currently works in the Ministry of Defence in Whitehall, London. He is a Fellow of the Society of Antiquaries of Scotland, but his archaeological interests extend well beyond Scotland, and include ancient Egypt and its hieroglyphic language as well as British archaeology in general. He is married and has two step-daughters and a step-son, all of whom are grown up, and two step-grandchildren.

Also available from **Thistle***Press*
Skye: The Complete Visitor's Guide
Gairloch & Torridon, The Complete Traveller's Guide To

Printed by BPC-AUP
Aberdeen, Scotland

CONTENTS

ACKNOWLEDGEMENTS

In writing this book, I have had to make use of the expertise and knowledge of many people, both on Skye and elsewhere. A complete list of their names, together with details of what they did, would require almost another book, so I hope that they will accept this general acknowledgement of my debt to them. But there is one person who must have a special mention: my wife, Elizabeth, whose idea this book was, and whose patience, help and encouragement kept it alive throughout all its gestation. In Skye she acted as note-taker, a scale for photographs used in compiling the site descriptions (as a sort of animated archaeological striped stick), and baggage carrier on all our explorations. Once warm and dry again, she proof read all my efforts and made innumerable helpful suggestions for improvements. Thus to her, and to everyone else who has contributed to this book, my most sincere thanks.

INTRODUCTION

S KYE is richly endowed with the archaeological signs and remains of its earlier inhabitants, with over a hundred prehistoric sites having been identified. For those who are used to carefully preserved ancient monuments, with clearly defined and signposted footpaths leading to them, a car park, an information centre selling souvenirs, and all the other trappings of the "Heritage" industry, the archaeological sites of Skye are, for the most part, going to be a surprise and even a disappointment. With the exception of Dun Beag at Struan, the evidence of the past inhabitants of the Island has been largely left to the mercy of the elements and, in days gone by, to anyone who needed some readily available quarried stone. As designated Ancient Monuments, they are no longer robbed and destroyed to provide the building materials for the people of the area but, in all too many cases, they receive little or no conservation, maintenance or repair.

The disadvantage of this state of affairs is that each Skye winter, with its winds and driving rain, further erodes the fabric, and each spring brings a surge in the growth of vegetation, loosening stones, blocking access and hiding details. But it is not all gloom and disaster. The wildness and isolation of most of the sites creates an atmosphere which can give the visitor the feeling of being far closer to the original inhabitants than is possible in the hurly-burly of those monuments elsewhere which have become modern tourist attractions. The difficulty in locating each site gives one a sense of achievement in reaching it, almost as if you were making an original discovery; then perhaps you are, in many ways, entering new territory, both in your knowledge of the past and of yourself. Sitting amongst the tumbled stones of a ruined broch or cairn with only the birds and rabbits as company and the silent majestic beauty of the Skye landscape all around, opens your mind to a greater understanding of the lives of the ancient peoples who left these memorials to their civilisation, and the tranquillity will allow Skye to work its healing magic as an oasis in the rush, noise and bustle of most of our daily lives.

I undertook this book in an attempt to make the archaeology of Skye a little more accessible to those whose time on the Island may well be all too brief. By describing, what I consider to be, the most interesting and better preserved sites, and giving, what I trust are, clear directions on how to reach them, I hoped to remove some of the frustrations and problems which arise when the exact location of a monument mentioned in the guidebook, or even marked on the map, is considerably less obvious on the ground. In so doing, I realise that, by increasing their popularity and accessibility, I run the risk of harming the monuments and their environment. For all those who wish to follow my directions, may I make a number of pleas in an attempt to ensure that you do not do anything which may cause damage to the structures or, by antagonising the owner of the land on which they stand, limit access for those who come later.

All the sites described in the subsequent pages are designated Ancient Monuments. Thus, any unauthorised excavation, the use of metal detectors, or the disturbance or removal of any object from the site, quite apart from being against the law and punishable by severe penalties, may well result in the irrevocable loss of a valuable piece in the jigsaw of our all too slender knowledge of the structures and the people who built them.

The land on which most of the monuments stand is privately owned and the notes in this book on how to reach the sites do not imply any public right of way. Before following these directions do, whenever practicable, seek the permission of the landowner and, in any case, ensure that you do not cause any damage to livestock, crops, gates, walls or fences. So please use gates, and shut them after you, or stiles, rather than climbing over walls and fences. If there is no alternative to climbing over a gate, then please do so as close to the hinges as possible, to reduce the risk of damage.

Also remember that much of Skye is given over to sheep farming, and sheep farmers, for very good reasons, do not like dogs (other than their own sheep dogs). Even the best behaved, and impeccably trained, town-bred dogs are quite likely, when faced with sheep, to find the instincts of their lupine ancestors irresistible. Many sheep farmers finding a dog worrying their stock will shoot it first and argue over the niceties later and, in many cases, will be legally entitled so to do. Probably the best advice I can give is: do not take your dog on your archaeological rambles, particularly in the lambing season. In fact, you will find many areas where there are prominent notices forbidding dogs and I would strongly urge you to comply with them. While on the subject of sheep, when you are driving remember that they are not over-endowed with road sense, especially when they are young. Keep your speed down and give yourself at least a chance of stopping when a sheep, apparently intent on suicide, jumps out almost under your front wheels, or has chosen to lie down on a nice warm piece of tarmac just beyond a completely blind corner.

In short, enjoy discovering more about the archaeology of Skye, relish the opportunity to walk surrounded by some of the most beautiful scenery in the world and take pleasure in the silence but, while doing so, remember all those whose livelihoods depend on the land over which you are walking and respect their property and livestock.

HISTORY

IN discussing prehistory, the terms Stone, Bronze and Iron Ages are frequently used to designate a period in time. While such terms provide a useful shorthand for indicating the period under discussion, they should not be regarded as tied to firm chronological dates. The spread of new technologies throughout Britain would have taken some time and it is entirely possible that man in such remote areas as the north west of Scotland would have been using stone implements, for example, well after his more advanced contemporaries further south were familiar with metal working.

Even in the more developed areas of Southern Europe, there can be similar anomalies such as that shown by the discovery in the Alps of the body of a man, whose remains can be dated to the a time usually considered to be within the Neolithic period. However, he was found to have been carrying a copper knife, demonstrating that metal may well have been in use, in at least that area, well before the time that had been previously supposed. It also shows that the divisions between the Ages spanned a large number of years, with a considerable amount of overlap and varying rates of progress in different regions. Nevertheless, provided the terms Stone, Bronze and Iron Ages are taken as indicating a sequence of development rather than fixed points in times, they are useful pointers.

In considering the prehistory of Skye, parallels are often drawn from archaeological evidence discovered elsewhere in the Western Isles and in mainland Scotland. While many such extrapolations from other areas will be valid, it needs to be borne in mind that there have been significant differences throughout history between Skye and other parts of Scotland. There is no reason to suppose that such local differences did not also exist in prehistoric times. There will have been contact between the prehistoric populations; indeed there is archaeological evidence for trade between regions geographically separated by considerable distances, but care is needed in basing assumptions on developments in Skye on evidence from elsewhere in Scotland, without collateral local supporting evidence. Having said that, there is still much investigation and excavation work needed in Skye to provide such supporting evidence and, in its absence, conclusions and theories have to be based on, what is in many cases, fairly slender archaeological data.

While the first signs of man in the south of Britain can be dated to as early as 500,000 BC, human activity in Scotland does not appear until some considerable time later. Indeed, even if man had ventured that far north, and there is no archaeological evidence to suggest that he did, the last Ice Age and its advancing glaciers would have driven him south again. It would not have been until well after those glaciers finally retreated by around 8,000 BC that Scotland and its islands would have been able to provide an environment suitable for man.

The first clear evidence of human activity in the Western Isles is stone implements found in Jura, which can be dated to about 5,500 BC. The large shell middens found in Coll indicate that, by about 4,500 BC, a large number of men were active there, although it can be argued that the shells could have been left by visiting gatherers/fishermen who lived further south and only came north in search of food. Whatever the correct interpretation of these finds, it can be assumed that, during the fifth millennium BC, a sizeable number of men regularly visited the islands, and may well have established some sort of community there.

Although it is entirely possible that Middle Stone Age man visited Skye in his hunt for food, he left little sign of his presence and there is no clear archaeological evidence of human habitation on the Island until well into the Neolithic period, although the recent discovery of a shell midden at Staffin may, once accurate dating has been completed, provide evidence of man's earlier presence on the island. Certainly man developed boats from a very early period and, while dug-out canoes would not have fared well on the seas around the Western Isles, craft constructed from animal skins stretched over wooden frames would have provided a much more seaworthy means of transport. Even with such relatively robust craft, the tide-rips and currents through narrows such as the Kyle of Lochalsh would have deterred the prehistoric sailors from using those routes, which could account for the earliest prehistoric remains not being located on the parts of Skye closest to the mainland.

In any case, groups of visiting hunter/gatherers, or even small established communities, would not necessarily leave much in the way of archaeological remains, and much of the evidence for their presence may still await discovery and identification. In addition, since their first areas of activity would almost certainly have been near the coast, changes in sea levels and subsequent coastal erosion may well have destroyed any signs which were left. While it is interesting to speculate on such matters, and important to acknowledge that there are still considerable gaps in our knowledge, it is safer to confine conclusions to matters which can be supported by hard archaeological evidence.

On that basis, the presence of chambered cairns on Skye show that, by the third millennium BC, the population of at least some areas of Skye had grown to the point where they were sizeable communities who had both the numbers and the necessary social structure to coordinate the efforts needed to construct these monuments. These men would have planted and harvested crops and may well have had domesticated cattle and sheep. Such food sources could have been supplemented by hunting and fishing. Unfortunately little is known about their dwellings, and many of the theories which have been advanced are based on assumptions developed from finds elsewhere in Britain. The lack of evidence of stone domestic structures could indicate that houses at this time were usually constructed of wooden frames with animal skins stretched over them; such light structures would leave little sign for the modern archaeologist, particularly where the land has later become covered with peat. Nor can we be sure who was buried in these cairns, although it is very doubtful that they could have provided the final resting place for everyone in a population of the size needed to provide the manpower to build them. This aspect is discussed in more detail later, in the section on chambered cairns.

The population of Skye probably continued to grow and communities were forced to seek new areas for their crops and domestic animals, as well as new hunting grounds for the creatures with which they supplemented their diet. This growing pressure on land and resources would seem to have begun to erode the peaceful co-existence which formed the basis of life in the second and third millennia BC. Whether it was such internal pressures, or as the result of incursions from elsewhere, there is clear evidence that, from about 1000 BC, communities began to need to provide fortifications to protect their people and, possibly, their domestic animals. All over Skye, stone-built fortifications begin to appear; some, like the promontory duns and hill forts, relying on natural features to provide part of their defensive strength; others like the duns and brochs relying on massive structures to give them some measure of impregnability. The evolution of such defensive works is both interesting and complex, and forms a later section in this book.

At about the same time as stone fortifications became common, stone domestic buildings were developed. Most of these were probably round in shape, as evidenced by the numerous hut circles which have been found from this period, but a rectangular Iron Age house has been discovered at Tungadal. Both types of houses probably had fairly low stone walls, with a pitched thatched or turfed roof supported on wooden beams. It is interesting to note that the house at Tungadal must have looked very similar to, albeit smaller than, the Skye Black Houses which were still in use in the last century, with examples to be seen today in the various folk museums around the Island, well over 2000 years after their predecessor. Associated with these domestic structures are the underground, stone-lined passage structures known, in Skye, as souterrains, but occurring elsewhere in Britain where they are also known as fogous or earth-houses. These structures are discussed in more detail later.

Although the current state of archaeological knowledge of the development of human activities in Skye is sufficient to signpost when man arrived and give some indication of how prehistoric man lived, there are considerable gaps in the story. Much remains to be done to build a complete picture of domestic architecture on the Island and to verify similarities and differences between what was happening on Skye and man's activities elsewhere in Scotland. A large number of sites have yet to be excavated and examined in detail, although much valuable work is being done by the Skye and Lochalsh Museum Service (Dualchas) and others.

CAIRNS, STANDING STONES, STONE CIRCLES AND HENGE MONUMENTS

CHAMBERED CAIRNS

Although Skye was undoubtedly populated in Neolithic times, there are few signs of man's presence which have survived until today. The only monuments which can be confidently assigned to the Neolithic period of the island's history are chambered tombs, of which Audrey Henshall lists six as being certain, with another four slightly more doubtful, as well as a possible long cairn. With the exception of the last mentioned, all the tombs, of which there are sufficient remains to permit classification, are of the Hebridean type, a form of passage-grave found on the North-west coast of Scotland and in the Hebrides. Most of the cairns are round or oval in plan, although there is one example of a square cairn at Carn Liath.

These Hebridean tombs usually consist of a stone-lined round or polygonal burial chamber, covered by a casing of stones piled up to give the cairn its domed shape and which can form a very large monument. The edge of this casing is often retained by a row of kerbing stones and the facade may be marked by larger stones, sometimes with a courtyard in front of the tomb. The chamber is connected to the outside of the casing by a short entrance passage; thus the chamber may well not be at the centre of the cairn. In some cairns, secondary burials in small stone-lined cells, known as cists, have been found. These may be later burials, perhaps reflecting some folk memory which led people to wish to be associated with what was seen as a sacred place from earlier times.

Very little work has been done on chambered cairns in Skye but they were probably used for successive burials over a fairly protracted period, with pottery vessels and stone objects included in the grave goods. They are unlikely to have been the burial places of a single chief or village head man, nor are they big enough, or sufficiently numerous, to have accommodated all the members of the community over the period during which they appear to have been in use. It is possible that they were used for members of the leading family of the community, or for the more distinguished citizens. It has also been suggested that remains may have been placed in the tomb for a period before being removed, as part of the funerary ritual, and re-buried elsewhere, although no subsidiary burials have been found to support this theory.

The remains of men, women and children have been found with the adults representing a wide range of ages within the context of the likely limited lifespan of Neolithic man. No complete skeletons have been found in the Skye tombs but it is not clear whether this is due to robbing and damage, or because it was the practice to disarticulate the skeletons before putting them in the tomb. It has been suggested, based on the evidence of Neolithic burials elsewhere in Scotland, that bodies were exposed to the air and, once the flesh had decayed or been devoured by birds of prey or other predators, only selected bones were placed in the tomb. Parallels for such practices have been drawn with the burial rites of the North American Indians, noted as recently as the last century.

Despite such speculations, it must be stressed that our knowledge of Neolithic burial customs is extremely incomplete and theories are based on limited archaeological evidence. It is tempting to read across from conclusions reached by examination of the much greater volume of remains in Orkney and elsewhere in Scotland, to base our assessments of the likely funerary practices in Skye. The customs and practices in historic times varied widely between the different regions of Scotland and, as has been noted earlier, there is no reason to suppose that such regional variations did not exist in prehistory.

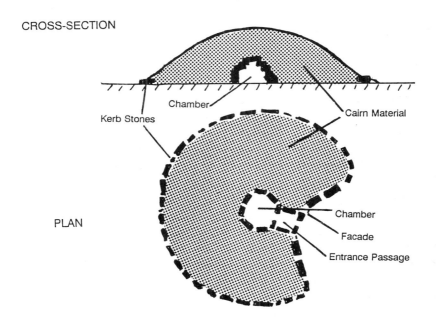

CROSS-SECTION

Chamber

Kerb Stones

Cairn Material

PLAN

Chamber

Facade

Entrance Passage

FEATURES OF A TYPICAL HEBRIDEAN CHAMBERED CAIRN

We can, however, safely conclude that the existence of chambered cairns in Skye shows that there was a well-established series of communities on the Island in Neolithic times and that they had the social structure and organisation to coordinate the efforts needed to build such large monuments. It would appear that, as happened elsewhere in Scotland, the practice of such monumental funerary arrangements fell into disuse and was probably replaced by individual burials sometime during the second millennium BC. Again, there is very little archaeological evidence to show what these new arrangements were, but it is clear that chambered cairns were not being built.

STANDING STONES, STONE CIRCLES AND HENGE MONUMENTS

Much more difficult to date than the chambered cairns, where burial customs and grave goods often provide a clear indication of when the monument was in use, are the standing stones, stone circles and henge monuments. Henge monuments usually consist of a ditch surrounded by an earth rampart, both of which are pierced by one or more entrance causeways. Since the ditch is usually inside the rampart, it is unlikely that these enclosures were defensive in nature and they probably represent some sort of gathering place for either religious purposes or for administrative reasons, such as councils, or possibly a combination of such uses.

Elsewhere in Britain, henge monuments often enclose stone circles; the best known examples of this type of monument are at Avebury and Stonehenge. In many cases, the henge was built first and the stone circles added at some later date. Although there is one certain, and two possible stone circles in Skye, and henge monuments are found throughout Britain from Cornwall to the Orkneys, there are no known henges on the Island. The reason for this absence is not known, although the generally hard rocks underlying shallow top soil would have made the digging of deep ditches extremely difficult, particularly using the usual horn implements. It could also be surmised that henge monuments were being built before settlement and organisation had reached a stage in Skye where such complex and labour intensive works could be undertaken. Equally, it could be argued that religious or political practices in Skye did not include the ceremonies or procedures which necessitated the use of such enclosures.

The purpose of stone circles is equally uncertain, with theories about their use as astronomical observatories and calculators for predicting eclipses having been put forward. While there is some evidence of circles and their outlying standing stones being based on alignment with the rising sun, or other astronomical features, the scale of effort required to transport and erect such monuments probably indicates that their primary purpose was religious or funerary. A parallel can possibly be drawn with the building of Europe's great cathedrals in medieval times, when such religious structures were on a scale which far exceeded that of contemporary secular building. Whatever the purpose of stone circles, the size of those in Skye is very much less than those found at Avebury or Stonehenge or even at Callanish in the Outer Hebrides. Again it is reasonable to assume that the scale of such monuments would have depended to a very large extent on the number of people available to undertake the work, with the degree of sophistication of the social organisation limiting how far this effort could be coordinated. From that assessment, it can be assumed that the communities in Skye at this period were still relatively small, and that joint ventures between adjacent communities were not generally undertaken, although similarities between the various classes of monuments indicate that there was contact between the communities on Skye, and with their neighbours on nearby islands and the mainland.

There are a number of standing stones on Skye, some being single stones and others in groups. But it should be remembered that not all standing stones are prehistoric in origin; in an area where large stone blocks are quite common, they are frequently erected for a wide range of purposes. I can remember, while driving in Shetland, seeing some very impressive standing stones by the roadside. Closer inspection revealed that each one had a small bronze plate recording that they had been erected by the Highways Commission to commemorate the opening of a new road. Stones have also been erected in historic times to mark boundaries, or even routes. Just to make everything more difficult to interpret, there are also examples of prehistoric stones being re-used at a later date. Despite such difficulties, dating of any organic remains found under the stone can give an indication of the date that the stone was put up and, on that basis, the standing stones detailed in this work are likely to have been prehistoric in origin. It is not only the dates of stones which can be ambiguous; their purpose and original form is also open to a great deal of discussion. For example, a single stone, or even a group of two or three stones, may well be the remains of a larger monument. They could be the sole remnants of a stone circle, or the outlying stones of such a monument, or they might always have been a single stone. In other cases, stone circles reported in older documents have disappeared; the circle at Kilbride in Skye is but one example. Detailed excavation can certainly give much additional information, including the original presence of other stones but, all too often, modern buildings and roads have erased much of the available evidence as well limiting the scope for excavation within anything approaching realistic costs.

All these limitations mean that making positive assertions about standing stones and stone circles is very difficult. Their function, original number and formation remains, in many cases, obscure. Their alignments have also given rise to innumerable theories ranging from maps of the stars to landing aids for visiting aliens, or astronomical calculators. Without wishing to get involved in controversial issues, it must be said that many of such theories are founded on minimal scientific facts. Certainly there appears to be a strong correlation between stone alignments and astronomical observations but whether such relationships reflect merely a convenient reference point for the building of these monuments, or the deep mystical significance attributed to them, is beyond resolution at our present state of knowledge. Nevertheless, speculation and discussion adds to the attraction of these essentially enigmatic monuments.

FORTIFICATIONS

MOST fortifications on Skye, in common with those throughout Scotland, are known as duns, from the Gaelic meaning a fort, regardless of how the archaeologist might wish to classify them. Even in archaeological terms the distinction between the various types is not entirely clear-cut, with various writers using different definitions. Thus, while the typical broch, dun or fort is fairly easy to recognise and classify, the boundaries between the types are open to argument. The problem is compounded when the structure has been heavily robbed of its stones and little is left but the foundations. Many structures, which may well have been brochs, for example, are now difficult to classify confidently as such, even after excavation; without the evidence from proper scientific examination, it is all too often impossible to be sure how the site should be described. In this book, the term broch is used to describe those structures which clearly exhibit the typical features of a broch as described later. Where there is insufficient evidence to be so confident, the structure will be described as a dun.

Even within the narrower definition used in this book, the term dun can cover a large range of different fortifications, ranging from relatively small round or oval structures with massive walls, through irregularly shaped enclosures, to large square or rectangular ones. There are also fortifications on promontories with a massive wall built across the neck of the land but with the precipitous cliffs forming the other three sides of the enclosure (although there would have been a light wall to guard against the occupants falling off). A further variation is where the wall of such promontory duns or forts is curved, sometimes to the point where it becomes semi-circular. These D-shaped promontory duns have been described as semi-brochs because their walls exhibit may of the typical broch features while not enclosing a complete circle. Even that description may not always be entirely unambiguous since, when a broch was built very close to the coast, as many were, later erosion can lead to part of the wall collapsing into the sea and what was a normal broch taking on the appearance of a semi-broch.

In order to provide a basis for classifying the various types in this book, dun is used to describe small (less than about 50 feet in diameter) circular or oval fortifications. Larger, square, rectangular or irregularly shaped structures are designated as forts. The terms promontory dun/fort are used where the main defences appear to have been a wall, ditch or rampart built across a promontory, but the cliffs or other natural features relied upon to provide defences on the other three sides. These terms are also used to cover the D-shaped semi-brochs. Other writers have used different demarcations, and sites described as one type in this book may well appear under a different heading elsewhere. Even within this book there will inevitably be occasions when a positive classification is not possible and many structures will exhibit characteristics of more than one category.

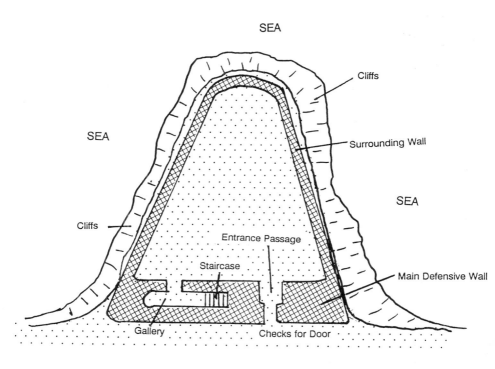

FEATURES OF A TYPICAL PROMONTORY DUN

DUNS

The first fortifications appear in Scotland around the middle of the first millennium BC with the earliest examples dating to between 700 and 600 BC. These early structures were generally small duns, either round or oval in plan with double rubble-filled walls tied together by timber ties. A number of these duns were destroyed by fire and the heat from the burning timbers melted the rubble filling in the walls into a solid mass, a process known as vitrification. The charcoal from the burnt timbers, thus preserved, provides the material for the radio-carbon dating of these structures. Later examples retained the double skin walls and rubble filling but replaced the timber ties with stone slabs. Dating of these structures has to rely on finds, or any organic material found near the foundations. There is thus a greater margin for error since it is difficult to be certain that such finds date from the earliest days of that structure. These small fortlets often incorporated a number of sophisticated features, including entrance passages with door checks and bar holes, as well as intramural galleries and cells. Some had staircases, set in the space between the double walls, presumably to give access to the top of the walls. It is possible, although by no means certain, that they were roofed with either stone or turfs but they may have merely had internal wooden structures built against the inside walls to provide some shelter for their occupants.

The duns are usually positioned on rocky knolls or other easily defended high points. It is clear that such positions were chosen primarily to improve the defensive strength of the dun but we know nothing of the attackers against whom they were intended to defend. It would seem that the earlier peaceful existence of the agrarian families and communities began to break down soon after the beginning of the first millennium BC but it is not known whether the threat was from outside invaders or as a result of growing populations putting increasing pressure on the land available for cultivation and the rearing of stock. Such pressures could well have led to attempts to wrest land and property from weaker neighbours, who responded by building these early fortifications to defend themselves, their families and their stock.

As already mentioned, there are some promontory duns, whose walls have a number of the features seen in a broch. E. W. MacKie has suggested that such structures could well be the precursors of the true brochs and that they should be known as semi-brochs. Radio-carbon dating of the promontory dun at Dun Ardtreck in Skye gave a date of 55 bc, which is hardly early enough to allow that dun to be regarded as being the basis for the development of the broch. The distribution of brochs in Skye does not really support the idea either since, as pointed out by Ann MacSween, brochs are concentrated in the northern half of the island, while the promontory duns occur in the south. That disparity in distribution would be strange if the promontory duns were the forebears of the brochs. However, much more damaging to the theory are the discoveries by Hedges and Bell at Bu in Orkney, which date the structures to 600 BC, some 500 years earlier than previously assumed for the development of brochs. On that evidence, it would appear that brochs first appeared in the Northern Isles before their building spread south to the Hebrides and the mainland of Scotland. This interpretation would place the semi-brochs as a variation, rather than the origin, of brochs. Development of the brochs continued, probably in parallel with the duns and other fortifications, in the Hebrides and on the Scottish mainland, but later examples of brochs in Orkney and Shetland became increasingly massive and probably taller, culminating in that at Mousa. While current evidence supports the progression outlined above, much more work, and accurate dating of the known brochs, is needed before the relative ages of these structures, and their place in the evolution of Scottish fortifications, can be definitively determined.

BROCHS

The broch is a type of fortification which is unique to Scotland and whose striking appearance and, in a few cases, spectacular remains, have resulted in a great deal being written about them. Unlike the other types of fortification discussed here, the brochs are a clearly defined group but, despite the many fine examples which exist, very little is known about their origins or their purpose. Even describing their primary purpose as defence entails a number of assumptions which would find those who strongly disagree.

The classic broch consists of a double walled dry-stone tower with a hollow space between its inner and outer walls, which are bound together by horizontal stone slabs, usually placed about every 3 to 5 feet. While the inner wall is vertical, the outer wall has an inward batter, giving the broch its characteristic shape similar to that of a modern power station cooling tower. In size, they vary surprisingly little, with an internal diameter of between 30 and 40 feet and wall base widths of between 9 and 15 feet. The best preserved example is at Mousa, in Shetland which, although it has lost its topmost courses, still stands to a height of over 38 feet and may well have been originally over 45 feet tall. Not quite as complete, nor as massive, but still very impressive and giving a clear idea of how brochs must have looked, are Dun Carloway on Lewis, and Dun Troddan and Dun Telve at Glenelg in Inverness-shire, which survive at their highest points to 40, 23 and 35 feet respectively.

There are the remains of 21 certain brochs surviving on Skye, all of which were probably built between about 100 BC and 100 AD. They almost invariably have a single entrance door set in a low passage, usually with checks for a door and holes for a locking bar, although the broch known as Dun Fiadhairt has two entrances. In many examples, there are one or more cells placed in the walls of this entrance passage, sometimes known as guard cells and intended perhaps to provide a refuge for defenders so as to enable them to enfilade any attackers who managed to penetrate the door. There is usually a staircase set in the cavity between the two walls, presumably giving access to upper galleries and possibly to the tops of the walls for look-out and defensive purposes although, since no broch has been found with the topmost courses of its walling intact, the existence of a rampart walkway must be conjectural. There are galleries set in the walls which could have been for storage, or as a place of safety for the women and children while their menfolk fought off any attackers who managed to penetrate into the body of the broch. The inner walls often have vertical gaps in their stonework, divided by stone slabs. These window-like apertures, known as voids, were, it has been suggested, to provide light in the spaces between the two walls. Since the inside surfaces of the walls are usually left rough finished, and the gaps between the two walls are very narrow, particularly towards their top, it is more likely that these intra-mural spaces were not used as rooms, and that the voids in the inner walls were intended to reduce the overall weight of the structure, particularly over the entrance to the broch, the access to the ground level galleries and to the stair case, and other weaker areas.

They would have also provided some light and ventilation for the staircase. Many of the brochs, notably Clickhimin in Shetland, have extensive outer defensive works but, in some cases, these may be later additions. Some brochs also have domestic buildings clustered around their walls. These too have been suggested as later additions but excavations at Howe in Orkney indicate that the broch and its surrounding houses were contemporaneous.

Why were the brochs built?

Although we know, to some extent, what brochs looked like, we are considerably less sure for what purpose they were built. It is unlikely that every broch was ever on the scale of that on Mousa but, even so, they are substantial structures requiring a great deal of skill and effort in their construction. Despite the uncertainty over their purpose, or possibly because of it, there are almost as many theories about the origins and purpose of the brochs as there are brochs themselves, but it must be remembered that they are theories with, in many cases, very little hard archaeological evidence to support or, for that matter, to disprove them. However, one can discount the more fanciful interpretations of the brochs' origins, such as they were built to resist the Roman invaders (brochs were being built well before the Romans landed in the South, let alone reached Scotland), or that they were Viking strongholds or Pictish pirate refuges. It is probable that, during their history, many brochs were used for some or all of those purposes but dating evidence clearly shows that the brochs were built well before the Romans arrived, or Vikings and Picts made use of them.

An alternative theory is that the brochs were built as signs of the strength and importance of the head of the family groups which owned them, rather as Norman castles were not only defensive works but also a clear and visible statement of the wealth and power of their owners. The existence of clusters of houses around the broch, as at Gurness and elsewhere, tends to support this idea of the broch being the centre of a group of families living in almost feudal awe of the broch owner. The corollary to this interpretation is that the broch would also provide a place of safety for the inhabitants of its associated community in times of trouble or attack, fulfilling a role similar to that of the Keep of a Norman castle. There are, however, a few problems with that interpretation. First the size of the broch, or to be more accurate, the size of the area enclosed by its walls: with an internal diameter of only some 30 to 40 feet, while there would have been space for permanent living quarters for a family, accommodating the inhabitants of even a small village would have been difficult. Added to which, the absence in most cases of any water supply or well within the broch's walls would have prevented it withstanding anything other than a short raid. Neither of these shortcomings would necessarily invalidate the idea of the broch fulfilling a similar role to that of a Norman Keep, if the threat were from lightly-armed raiders who attacked with little or no warning, relying on surprise to achieve their aims, but having neither the desire, nor the capability, to undertake a protracted siege. The strength of the broch, its height, its usual single, very constricted entrance and lack of window openings together with, in many cases, extensive outworks all point to it having a defensive role, but its other limitations indicate that this role was essentially short-term.

The idea of brochs being the prehistoric equivalents of Norman castles is undermined, to some extent, by the lack at many broch sites of any evidence of associated domestic buildings outside the broch walls. Perhaps the safest interpretation is to regard the brochs as fortified homesteads around which, in some cases, villages sprang up, with the inhabitants possibly trusting that the obvious strength of the broch would act as a deterrent or, if that failed, the broch would provide some form of refuge. In other words, the broch may have fulfilled the role of the Keep in later fortifications, as the last refuge against attackers but, in the case of the broch, against an attacker who was expected to carry out a hit-and-run raid rather than undertake a protracted siege. The problems with this interpretation are the identity of these raiders and the lack of archaeological evidence of brochs coming under attack. One could argue that the value of the broch as a deterrent persuaded potential raiders to direct their efforts against softer targets and, thus, that the very success of the broch has resulted in a lack of evidence to prove its role.

As far as the attackers are concerned, we are on even less solid ground. The location of most brochs near the coast, generally close to flat fertile areas suitable for farming (as Ann MacSween has pointed out, on Skye only three of the 21 certain brochs are more than a mile from the shore, and only six are on land which is of questionable value today for either grazing or agriculture), has been suggested as indicating that they were the response of a predominately agricultural community to a threat of seaborne attack. Such ideas would account for the broch often being built on low ground rather than on a nearby, more commanding, defensive position. If the raids which these peoples feared were seaborne, warning times would have been short and the broch would have needed to be very close to where the community worked in the fields, so that the people, and possibly their animals, could be secured within its walls in the short time available before the raiders were upon them. While there is no hard evidence for the existence of such marauding corsairs, the later history of Scotland is full of sudden attacks by clans on their neighbours, often using boats to achieve surprise. Are the brochs the silent memorials of earlier, pre-clan, strife? Certainly the time and effort required to build them indicates that the community considered that they were a worthwhile investment, either in protection or prestige.

Broch Construction

The enigma of the brochs does not end with the consideration of their purpose; their construction and internal arrangements are also problematic. Even the best preserved brochs, such as that at Mousa in Shetland, are simply dry-stone towers with, usually, no sign of internal divisions. Many brochs, including those at Midhowe and Gurness in Orkney, have stone partitions within their walls, giving them the appearance of the later, and much less massive, domestic buildings known as wheel-houses, but these arrangements are far from typical. They have been explained, in the past, as later additions, but the stone internal divisions at Bu broch were almost certainly put in when the broch was originally built. Again the discoveries at Bu call into question previously accepted ideas on brochs and perhaps indicate that there was a greater disparity in their individual designs than had been supposed.

Most brochs have one or more ledges, known as scarcements, around their inner walls. These have been suggested as indicating that the broch had internal floors and, extrapolating from that conclusion, must also have been roofed. As no broch retains its topmost courses of stones today, it is difficult to be positive about the existence of roofs but the lack of sockets in the walls for the fairly considerable beams, which would have been needed to support the lower floors, casts some doubt on the idea that the brochs had such internal arrangements. Added to which, the lower scarcements are sometimes no more than three or four feet above the ground level. A floor at that height would seem to be of little use and the lack of space beneath it would have severely restricted defence if the entrance door had been breached by attackers.

A more attractive theory is that, while some brochs had internal divisions built of stones, others may have had one or more wooden verandah-like structures, based on the scarcements, built round the inside of its walls. These could have been roofed to protect the occupants from the elements, or from any missiles launched over the walls by attackers. Such verandahs would not have needed heavy beams to support them, and thus the absence of beam sockets in the walls is not an obstacle. Without such substantial beams, the verandas would certainly have needed some form of pillars to support their internal edges. The discovery of a series of concentric postholes at some brochs could well have been the remains of these supporting pillars, but it must be said that such postholes are by no means universal, nor can they be positively ruled out as later additions. Thus, as with so much about the brochs, we cannot be positive about their internal arrangements, nor whether or not they were roofed. The best one can say is that the theory, which has been put forward, that they were topped with dry-stone domes, although probably technically feasible is, at best, highly conjectural.

It has also been suggested that the superficial consistency of the design of the brochs, and the relatively short period within which they were thought to have appeared, indicates that they were constructed by a group of itinerant builders who provided local chieftains with a bespoke defensive system. The revisions to the dating of brochs, necessitated by the discoveries at Bu, make that theory less attractive, as does the fact, discussed earlier, that although brochs share a number of common features, there are sufficient variations in their individual architectural features to rule out the idea of their having been built to a common pattern. There are also clear signs of evolution in their design. Some brochs, including all those on Skye, were built with galleries in their walls at ground level, while other, possibly later, designs employed a solid base. It is attractive to speculate that the hollow based brochs proved to be less robust than their solid based counterparts and thus the solid base became the preferred design. At Midhowe in Orkney, the original galleries in the base of the broch have been partly filled, and the outer walls buttressed, perhaps indicating that, at some time in its early history, it showed signs of structural weakness and had to be reinforced. Similarly, at Gurness, also in Orkney, there are signs of the galleries in the base of the broch having been crushed by the weight of the superstructure. Such occurrences could tend to support the theory that hollow-based brochs were less successful than the solid based ones, but the evidence, it must be admitted, is far from conclusive.

Certainly the brochs on Skye are generally less massive than those on the Northern Isles. In her survey of the fortifications on Skye, Ann MacSween points out that of the nineteen brochs which could be measured, out of the total of twenty-one on Skye, the ratio of the thickness of their walls to the diameter of their bases is less than 50%, while well over half of the northern brochs have ratios greater than 50%. This difference could also indicate that the Skye brochs were probably not as high as those on the Northern Isles. Perhaps attempts to increase the height at Midhowe and Gurness, while retaining the ground level galleries and less massive wall structure, similar to the Skye brochs, led to the problems noted above.

Whatever the progression in the developments of the bases of the brochs, it is reasonable to suppose that the hollow walls were designed to provide greater height than would have been practicable with a solid construction. That interpretation begs the question of why it became necessary to build such high structures, rather than more squat, and thus easier to build, fortifications. Assuming that the primary purpose of the brochs was defence, the development of more sophisticated weapons by the likely attackers, giving them the capability of launching projectiles over lower walls, could be one reason but, without collateral evidence, such explanations can only be surmise. Continuing investigation of the brochs is adding to our knowledge and many former theories of their place in Scottish history have had to be modified in the light of recent discoveries. It is probably safest to regard the brochs as but one response to the need for fortifications and that they developed in parallel with the other forms. Their origins are obscure but the peak of broch building appears to have occurred around 100 BC but even then they did not replace the other forms. In different areas of Scotland, different solutions were found to the problem of ensuring the security of the family, or community, against attack. The broch, the dun, the fort and the promontory dun should be regarded as parallel developments rather than the stages in a progression. Nevertheless, the broch is undoubtedly the most sophisticated, and impressive, form of such prehistoric fortifications. Its construction, with double walls and gaps in the inner ones, seems to have been directed towards producing an extremely strong, tall structure using the minimum amount of materials, and restricting the overall weight of the building. The survival of many of these monuments until the present day is a dramatic indication of their strength and durability.

Remains of Brochs

Although there are remains of at least twenty-one brochs on Skye, the most impressive surviving brochs are found elsewhere, and thus lie outside the scope of this book. Nevertheless, those interested in seeing more complete examples than are available on Skye, should try to find the time to take the Kylerhea ferry across to Glenelg and look at Dun Telve and Dun Troddan which are well signposted and situated beside the road about 5 miles from the ferry. These two brochs, while neither as large nor complete as Dun Carloway on Lewis or Mousa on Shetland, remain standing to 35 and 23 feet respectively at their highest points. They are a most impressive reminder of what the Skye brochs could have looked like. They also include, in more complete form, many of the broch characteristics which, with a little care, can still be identified in their more ruinous neighbours on Skye.

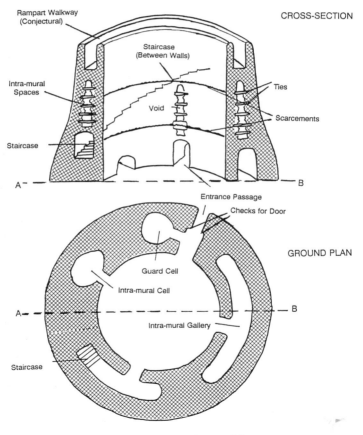

FEATURES OF A TYPICAL BROCH

SOUTERRAINS

SOUTERRAINS occur widely throughout the British Isles, although they are known by a number of different names in different regions, including Fogous in Cornwall and Earth Houses in the Northern Isles. Their designs vary but they generally consist of a stone-lined passage, often dug into the side of a hill or mound, and sometimes with a cell at the far end. The earth houses in Orkney are more elaborate than most, often with a flight of steps leading down to an entrance passage which opens into a pillared chamber cut out of the rock. The surviving examples in Skye are simpler and less deeply buried than their northern neighbours, consisting of just a low passage, with only that at Ullinish showing any sign of a cell at its end.

Their purpose is not entirely clear but they are almost invariably associated with domestic structures. In the case of the souterrain at Tungadal, it appears to be an integral part of the house there. The Rennibister earth house in Orkney when first discovered was found to be filled with human bones from 6 adults and 12 children, all of which had been disarticulated and thus probably placed in the earth house as bones, rather than as complete bodies. Despite that find, it is most unlikely that the original purpose of these structures was funerary. Nor is it likely that they were fortifications. It has been suggested that they might have been used to provide a last refuge when the community was under attack but, quite apart from their dimensions making them incredibly cramped for this purpose, the single entrance would have made them a death trap since a fire lit there would have quickly either suffocated the occupants or forced them to emerge.

It has also been suggested that they were a secure hiding place for valuables but it is difficult to see why, if that was their purpose, their passages should have been made 20 feet or more long when a much shorter and more easily constructed design would have provided the same amount of protection and concealment. As with the bones mentioned above, it may well have been that souterrains were sometimes used to hide valuables but that was probably not the purpose for which they were originally built.

A possible explanation of their purpose is that they were used for the storage of food. The long passage would have been necessary to ensure that the storage area was well away from the entrance so that an even temperature would be maintained. This interpretation would also account for the small size of the passage (usually about 3 feet square) since a narrow and low roofed passage would contribute to maintaining an even temperature by limiting the amount of air movement each time the souterrain was opened to place in, or take out, supplies. The carefully constructed stone lining of the passages would also indicate that they were intended for regular, prolonged use, rather than to meet occasional emergency purposes when a less elaborate and easier to build structure would have sufficed. Certainly, a stone lining would have been essential if grain or other food stored in the souterrain were not to suffer damage from water, or attacks from mice and other rodents. Indeed, some form of secondary protection might well have also been necessary. At the risk of venturing into the realms of conjecture, it is possible to suggest that covered baskets, perhaps lined with large leaves, when placed in the stone chambers whose entrances were then sealed, would have provided a practicable means of storing food for quite protracted periods.

A fogou in Cornwall has been found with a chamber at the end of its passage which appears to have been used for storing grain. If this structure was intended to be used as an underground silo, some form of lining would be essential to keep the grain dry and thus preventing it germinating, but a stone-lined cell with perhaps an additional wicker lining or large baskets would be effective. Although no remains of any such internal arrangements have been found so far, the link with food storage provided by this case may well be an insight into the purpose of these structures elsewhere.

While it is not possible to make any categoric statement about the purpose of the Skye souterrains, or indeed the examples of similar structures elsewhere in Britain, their use as a prehistoric larder seems to be consistent with the archaeological evidence available. To venture into discussions about their possible use as ice-houses, where ice cut in the winter was stored to keep food cold in the summer, while a practice common in historical times and thus perfectly feasible, would be extrapolating from the available evidence to an unjustified degree.

LAYOUT OF LIST OF SITES

THE monuments listed in the following pages are grouped into four regions, as shown on the map on the next page. The two northern regions comprise that part of Skye which lies north of a line drawn from Portree due west across the Island to the west coast. This area is further divided into the North West and North East Regions by a line drawn due south from Lyndale Point between Loch Greshornish and Loch Snizort to the southern boundary of the area. Thus the North West Region includes Waternish and Duirinish, while the North East Region consists mainly of the Trotternish peninsula. The Central Region lies between the southern boundary of the northern area and a line joining the head of Loch Ainort on the north coast, to that of Loch Scavaig on the south. This Region includes Minginish and the Cuillin areas. The fourth area, designated the Southern Region, is that part of Skye which lies south and east of the southern boundary of the Central Region, and thus includes the Sleat and Strath peninsulas as well as the south-east corner of the Island. Within those regions, the sites are listed broadly in the order that they would be reached travelling from Portree.

Each entry includes the OS map reference of the site, together with brief notes on the monument's state of preservation and main points of interest, followed by detailed directions on how to find it. The time quoted against each set of directions is an estimate of how long it will take you to walk to the monument, examine its main features and then walk back to where you have parked your car. Obviously, such times will vary considerably, depending on your walking speed and, more significantly, the time you wish to spend looking at the monument. As noted in the directions, visiting some sites requires quite long walks across rough country but none requires climbing, difficult scrambling or more than average fitness to complete (otherwise I would not have got to them). Having said that, very few indeed of the sites are accessible to anyone who has to use a wheelchair or is otherwise unable to walk over rough ground. Where sites can be clearly viewed from the road, for example the Borve Standing Stones, the Ullinish chambered cairn and, at slightly longer range, Dun Hallin and Dun Beag, this fact is included in the site notes.

Finally, it is probably worth pointing out again that these directions do not imply any public right of way or right of access and that, wherever possible, the owner's permission should be sought before setting off across private land. May I also re-stress the need to ensure that you do not disturb livestock, particularly sheep during the lambing season, and take every care not to damage walls or gates.

ISLE OF SKYE: *Showing the Regions under which the Sites are listed*

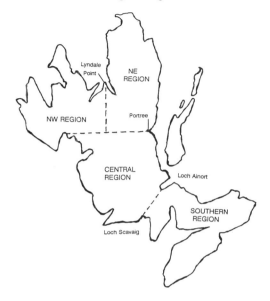

NORTH EAST REGION
Dun Gerashader (Fort)
Dun Torvaig (Fort)
Clachan Erisco (Standing Stones)
Kensaleyre (Cairn and Standing Stones)
Dun Eyre (Fort)
Dun Adhamh (Aidh)(Fort)
Kingsburgh (Broch)
Dun Santavaig (Fort)
Dun Maraig (Fort)
Uig (Standing Stones)
Dun Skudiburgh (Fort)
Dun Liath (Fort)
Dun Flodigarry (Broch)
Dun Suledale (Broch)

NORTH WEST REGION
Dun Hallin (Broch)
Dun Borrafiach (Broch)
Dun Gearymore (Broch)
Dun Fiadhairt (Broch)
Claigan (Souterrain)
Dun Osdale (Broch)
Dun Chaich (Fort)
Dun Totaig (Fort)
Dun Boreraig (Dunvegan) (Broch)
Dun Colbost (Broch)

CENTRAL REGION
Dunan an Aisilidh (Dun)
Dun Diarmaid (Dun)
Dun Beag (Broch)
Dun Mor (Fort)
Cnoc Ullinish (Souterrain)
Cnoc Ullinish (Chambered Cairn)
Tungadal (House and Souterrain)
Dun Feorlig (Dun)
Vatten (Chambered Cairns)
Dun Ardtreck (Semi-broch)
Rudh an Dunain (Chambered Cairn and
       Promontory Dun)
Dun Sleadale (Broch)
Ard an T'Sabhail (Broch)

SOUTHERN REGION
Liveras (Chambered Cairn)
Achadh A'Chuim (Chambered Cairn)
Clach na H'Annait (Standing Stone)
Dun Ringill (Semi-broch)
Cnocan nan Gobhar (Chambered Cairn)
Na Clachan Bhreige (Stone Circle)
Allt na Cille (Souterrain)
Dun Grugaig (Promontory Fort)

NORTH EAST REGION

DUN GERASHADER
(Map Ref: NG 489452)

Dun Gerashader is clearly visible from the main Portree to Staffin road, situated on the northern end of a rocky ridge which has steep, and in places precipitous, sides. This fort, which measures 160 feet by 90 feet, is similar in design to a promontory fort in that its main defences are built across the ridge, with a lighter wall supplementing the natural defences provided by the rocky slopes on the other three sides. The lighter wall has largely disappeared but the main wall still exists up to about 12 feet in height, and about 14 feet in thickness, although in part obscured by fallen stones. There are two clearly defined entrances on the east side and signs of a third on the west. In front of the main defensive wall there are four rows of boulders set on edge across the ridge, the outer two of which are built from one side of the ridge to the other, while the inner two are built from the western edge of the ridge to a rocky outcrop about halfway across. These boulders were presumably intended to act as an obstacle to attackers approaching the fort along the ridge, and were thus similar in function to the "Chevaux de Frise" used in later defensive works although, unlike their later counterparts, not intended to impede attacks by cavalry.

Directions
(Time: 30 minutes)

The fort is most easily reached from the minor road, signposted to Torvaig, which turns off to the right from the Portree to Staffin road (A855) about one mile outside Portree. Parking is not easy, but there are a few places beside the main road where you can leave your car without obstructing traffic or access to the fields. The route is across land that can be very wet and boggy and is criss-crossed with small streams and ditches, so waterproof boots are advisable. Cross the field to the right of the Torvaig road and climb up the hill to the left of the fort, which you will see at the right-hand end of the ridge, so as to approach it up the slope from the south-east.

DUN TORVAIG
(Map Ref: NG 494442)

Like the previous site, Dun Gerashader, Dun Torvaig is similar in design to a promontory fort, except that it is located on an inland ridge rather than a headland. This oval-shaped fort measures about 65 feet by 50 feet and has two main defensive walls built across the ridge and a lighter wall enclosing the other three sides. The inner main wall is largely obscured by a mass of fallen stones about 30 feet wide and rising to about 6 feet in height. A short section of walling survives amidst this debris. The outer main defences consisted of a

double wall, the faces of which were about 3 feet in width and 10 feet apart. There are signs of an entrance towards the southern end of these outer walls but the corresponding entrance through the inner wall has disappeared.

Directions   (Time: 45 minutes)

From the Portree to Staffin road (A855), turn right about one mile outside Portree on to the minor road signposted to Torvaig. Follow this road for just over one mile, round two right-hand bends, until just before it ends in a works site. There is space to park on the right of the road after passing a farm and bungalow on the left. The fort is visible on the skyline on top of a rocky outcrop on the ridge to the left of the road. Walk back up the road and enter the field on your right through the gate immediately next to the cowshed. Cross the wooden bridge which spans the small stream and make for the drystone wall at the opposite end of the field. Climb over this wall, taking care not to dislodge its stones, and head up the hill towards the rocky cliffs. At the base of these cliffs, turn right and, keeping them to your left, walk round until they become less steep. Then turn up the hill towards the fort, approaching it from the south-west.

CLACHAN ERISCO STANDING STONES   (Map Ref: NG 452480)

The Clachan Erisco standing stones at Borve are the only prehistoric remains on Skye which you can, if you so wish, examine closely without getting out of your car. The three stones stand in a slightly curving line on the grass verge beside the road about 8 feet apart. Two of the stones are 5 feet in height while the third is a little under 3 feet. It has been suggested that these stones may be part of a large stone circle, and large monoliths, which could have been part of such a circle, have been found built into nearby walls. Assuming that this monument was originally a true circle, and extrapolating from the arc formed by the remaining three stones, it would have been of considerable size.

Directions

On the Portree to Uig road (A856) close to where the road to Dunvegan (A850) branches off to the left are, in succession, three minor roads, all signposted to Borve, which turn off the main road on its right-hand side. It does not matter which of these turnings you take, but the first one you come to on the way from Portree is the closest to the Stones. Follow this minor road as it winds up the hill until it turns left to parallel the main road. The stones are on the roadside verge on the left of the road, 350 yards from that turn. Continuing along the road will bring you to the second and third turnings which lead back to the main road.

KENSALEYRE CHAMBERED CAIRN (CARN LIATH) AND STANDING STONES

(Map Refs: Cairn NG 420514, Stones NG 414525)

The cairn, which is visible from the Portree-Uig road (A856), is in a fairly ruinous condition, consisting of a pile of small water-worn stones, now partly turf covered, some 18 feet high and about 80 feet in diameter. There are two large stones exposed in the SSW face of the cairn, which may be the remains of an entrance passage, but there are no signs of its further structure; nor is it possible to enter the chamber. On the north-east side of the cairn, about half way up, some displaced flattish stones are all that remains of a cist, found in 1907 by some men looking for a large stone for a lintel. Finding human bones, which have since disappeared, they desisted in their efforts. If you look North from the cairn, you will be able to see, across the bay and about a mile away, two standing stones which align precisely with the cairn's entrance. This alignment may be entirely fortuitous since there is no evidence to support the view that the cairn and standing stones are contemporaneous. Nevertheless, it is at least an interesting coincidence.

Directions

(Time: 1 hour)

On the Portree to Uig road (A856), two and a half miles after the Dunvegan road (A850) joins it from the left, park your car on the remains of the old road opposite a small disused chapel and the minor road signposted to Keistle and Rhenetra. Enter the field through the nearby gate and make your way towards the cairn. The field is often very marshy and is criss-crossed by ditches and rivulets, so waterproof boots are advisable. You can take a closer look at the standing stones by returning to your car and driving threequarters of a mile further along the A856 towards Uig, when you will be able to see the stones on the far side of the field on the left. Park in the lay-by and enter the field through the gate. Walk down the hill towards the stones which are clearly visible ahead of you. At the cairn and the standing stones, be particularly careful about shutting the gates behind you, both on your way to the sites and when you return to your car. The fields are frequently used for grazing bullocks, and the main Portree-Uig road is no place for young cattle to wander.

DUN EYRE

(Map Ref: NG 420535)

Dun Eyre stands on a rocky plateau, which measures 100 feet by 58 feet and whose cliffs rise between 10 and 20 feet above the surrounding moorland. There are not sufficient remains of the walls visible to be sure of the size of this fort but it is probable that it occupied the whole of the plateau, thus making use of the cliffs to supplement its defences. The defences are better preserved at the southern end of the fort where there is a double wall which curves round the edge of the plateau, with the outer wall faced with boulders, and an entrance through both walls set in the centre. An interesting and unusual feature is the double row of boulders set on end, 4 to 6 feet apart, for a distance of about 60 feet from this wall, forming what may be described as a processional way up to the main entrance of the fort.

Directions (Time: 40 minutes)

From the Portree to Uig road (A856), about 7 miles from Portree, turn right on to the minor road on the right, signposted to Eyre. Drive to the end of this road and park there, making sure that you do not obstruct access to the fields and farm workings. The fort is visible on the skyline about 600 yards straight ahead in the direction of the road. Continue in the same direction as the road, keeping the fence on your left, and go through two gates. Immediately after the second of these, turn right up the hill between the wire fence and the old stone wall. Cross the fence ahead of you and continue up the steep hill towards the large rocky plateau slightly to your left. The entrance to the fort, with its "processional way", is on the right-hand side of this plateau. This is not a difficult walk but the ground near the last fence is crossed by a stream and can be very marshy.

DUN ADHAMH (AIDH) (Map Ref: NG 411546)

Dun Adhamh, which is also known as Dun Aidh, occupies an oval plateau about 50 feet above the surrounding moorland. The fort, which is very roughly rectangular in shape, measures 94 feet by 40 feet, with walls about 10 feet thick which are best preserved on the eastern side where they are 18 inches high. There is a clearly defined entrance at the south-east end, to the north of which, in the north-east corner of the fort where the wall bulges outwards, there are the remains of a semi-circular structure built against the wall. It is interesting to speculate that this structure could have been similar to the drop-shaped building which can be seen, in more complete form, at Dun Skudiburgh, although that comparison does nothing to resolve what the purpose of these structures might have been, nor is it by any means certain that the structure here was similar to the Skudiburgh one. Outside the north-western end of the fort, about 60 feet from the wall, are the remains of an earthen rampart 9 feet broad, which survives to a height of about 2 feet. There is a break in this rampart, opposite the northern corner of the fort, in which there are the remains of a circular stone structure about 6 feet in diameter on top of a mound. While the rampart was almost certainly a defensive feature, the purpose of the small circular structure is unclear.

Directions (Time: 40 minutes)

From the Portree to Uig road (A856), about eight and a half miles from Portree, there is a turn on the left signposted to Romesdal. A third of a mile further on, there is a sign to Iulan Dubh Bed and Breakfast, beside which is a parking area formed from the old road. Park your car in that area, from which the fort is visible in the middle distance as a tumble of fallen stones on a rocky eminence. Walk 30 yards up the main road towards Uig, to a gate on the right. Go through that gate and cross the moorland at right angles to the road in an ENE direction for about 700 yards, crossing a small ridge and then climbing up the hill to the fort. The terrain is quite rough in places, with very wet marshy ground and numerous ditches. In anything other than the driest weather, good waterproof boots are advisable and, even with them, completing the visit dry-shod cannot be guaranteed unless you are very careful where you put your feet.

KINGSBURGH BROCH
(Map Ref: NG 389569)

The broch at Kingsburgh has an outside diameter of about 57 feet with walls about 12 feet in thickness. Although the broch is very ruined, both the inner and outer faces of its walls can be traced, and remain in places up to 4 feet high on the outside. There is a clearly defined entrance passage in the northern sector with what may be a door check on the right-hand side. A gallery, the entrance to which is in the south part of the inner wall, almost opposite the entrance passage, runs round within almost the entire perimeter of the walls, except for the sector either side of the entrance passage. There is no sign of any guard cell. Inside the broch are the remains of a circular structure about 18 feet in diameter, built against the south wall. This structure may well indicate the use of the broch as a domestic dwelling after its main defensive purpose had lapsed. Such interpretation is supported by the extensive remains of domestic and farm buildings scattered around the site of the broch.

Directions
(Time: 90 minutes)

From the Portree to Uig road (A856), about 9 miles from Portree, go past the turning to the left, signposted to Kingsburgh, and continue for just less than another mile, until there is a wooded plantation on the right. Opposite the far side of that plantation, there is a farm track on the left with farm buildings and a house to the left of it. There is room to park on the left-hand verge just beyond that track. Walk down the track, through the right-hand gate of the three you will see ahead of you, and along the track, which can be very muddy in wet weather, across a small wooden bridge and through a second gate. Continue along the track for about another half a mile, crossing a second smaller stream over the stone culvert. When the track begins to bear left and starts to descend gently towards the shore, you will see on the left a T-shaped stone dyke. Turn left and walk up the hill, parallel to the vertical of the T and cross its horizontal bar towards the rocky ridge that you will see ahead of you. Kingsburgh Broch is at the top of this ridge at its southern end.

DUN SANTAVAIG
(Map Ref: NG 383572)

Dun Santavaig is a very large fort indeed, measuring about 350 feet by 180 feet, although the whole perimeter may not have been enclosed by walls but may have relied on the sheer cliffs on its northern and north-western sides to provide adequate defence. The main defensive wall is built across the ridge, in a north-easterly direction from the edge of the cliff in the south-west corner of the fort for 30 yards, and then northwards along the eastern edge for a further 60 yards until the height and steepness of the side of the ridge would have provided adequate defensive strength. The lower courses of the wall across the ridge are still visible, although the rest has been reduced to a tumble of fallen stones. There is an entrance passage about 10 feet wide in this wall, with signs of a short stretch of outer defensive wall opposite it, running parallel to the main one about 18 feet further to the south-east.

Directions   (Time: Add 45 minutes to Kingsburgh time)

After leaving Kingsburgh broch, return to the track and continue along it until just before it reaches the shore. About 100 yards short of the beach, turn right and strike up the hill, between the two rocky knolls which you will see ahead of you. The south wall of the fort appears as a tumble of fallen stones along the edge of the hill immediately in front of you. It is well worth climbing to the top of the high ground at the far end of the fort for, on a clear day, the truly magnificent views from the Outer Hebrides in the north to the Cuillins in the south. The remains of the medieval castle, Caistel Uisdein (Hugh's Castle) are also clearly visible on the coast to the north.

DUN MARAIG (CUIDRACH)   (Map Ref: NG 377592)

Dun Maraig occupies the whole of a small tidal islet 70 yards from the end of the headland which forms the western side of the bay, Poll na h'Ealaidh, on the eastern shore of Loch Snizort. This fort is very roughly oval in shape, measuring about 120 feet by 60 feet. Very little of its walling now survives but it is of interest since it is the only example on Skye of a defended island. It is thus similar in concept to the crannogs which occur elsewhere in Scotland although, unlike a crannog, the island on which it is based is an entirely natural feature, rather than being man-made. Originally, the islet was joined to the shore by a causeway, now completely destroyed.

Directions   (Time: 90 minutes)

From the Portree to Uig road (A856), about 13 miles from Portree, turn left down the minor road, signposted to Cuidrach. As this road nears the coast, take the left fork and continue to just before it ends. Parking is not easy but there is a turning space on the left which is large enough to permit one smallish car to be parked there without obstructing its primary purpose. The fort is on the small islet at the end of the headland across the bay. Walk to the end of the road and then continue along the track that branches off it slightly to the left, keeping the fence and wall on your right. Do not be tempted to take a short cut across the fields since the numerous fences and ditches which cross them make that route one of the many instances on Skye where the shortest distance between two points is not a straight line. After 700 yards, there is a dry-stone sheep fank on the right. Turn right there and make your way round the bay to the small islet, just off the end of the point. Although the islet was originally joined to the mainland by a causeway, this no longer exists and the fort is accessible only at low tide.

UIG STANDING STONES
(Map Ref: NG 394628)

One stone remains standing and there is the stump of a second stone, 3 feet away, with small stones used as wedges at its base. In the survey of monuments carried out by the Royal Commission on Ancient and Historic Monuments of Scotland in 1928, both stones are reported to be fallen, so the one now standing has been re-erected in modern times. Both stand on top of a mound which is about 100 yards from the road. When I visited this site in 1991, wild flowers had been strewn around the base of the standing stone which tempted me to think of surviving folk memories of early worship. However, I suspect that activities of the children from the nearby school are a more likely, even if more prosaic, explanation.

Directions
(Time: 20 minutes)

On the road from Portree to Uig (A856), about one mile before entering Uig, on the hill leading down to the town, just before the 40 mph limit signs, there is a house on the right, next door to a school. Immediately up the hill from this house is an old loading platform with a small iron gate to the right of it. There is just room to park one car beside this platform, without obstructing the entrance to the house. Park there and go through the iron gate, turn half right and walk up the steep hill towards an electricity pole at the top. The stones stand on top of a raised mound which is about 100 yards from the gate, surrounded by old field enclosures.

DUN SKUDIBURGH
(Map Ref: NG 374647)

Dun Skudiburgh is a fairly complex defensive structure which, although much of its original walling has disappeared, still shows some interesting and unusual features. These features, the pleasant walk needed to reach it and, like so many of the sites on the west coast of Trotternish, the beautiful coastal views from its summit, make this a site well worth visiting. The roughly oval-shaped fort, measuring 160 feet by 130 feet, consisted of a wall about 10 feet thick, built close to the edge of the small plateau on which it stands. This wall has almost entirely disappeared. Against what would have been the inner face of this wall, on its eastern side, there is a small drop-shaped dry-stone building, 35 feet long and 25 feet wide, the wall of which still exists to a height of 9 feet in places. Outside the south-western side of this building is a short length of dry-stone walling about 4 feet high, built parallel to, and some 3 feet from, its wall. It appears to be a very recent addition, which is not mentioned in earlier descriptions of this site, but why anyone should have built it is unclear. There is no sign of an entrance to the drop-shaped building from inside, or outside, the fort enclosure and its purpose is obscure. It is tempting to interpret this structure as some form of lookout tower, perhaps reached by a ladder from inside the fort, or even as fulfilling a similar function to that of a keep in a Norman castle, although its small size does not really support that interpretation. In any case, such ideas are, at best, conjectural.

The fort was further protected by an outer wall built below it on the landward side, starting from the cliff south-east of the fort and continuing in a gentle curve northwards along the eastern edge of the ridge for 100 yards. The southern part of this wall has been destroyed but the northern sector is clearly visible. At the northern end of this wall is an entrance, and then the outer wall continues in a SSW direction towards the cliffs on the seaward side, forming a triangular lower courtyard. Between this courtyard and the fort, running roughly east to west, is an inner cross wall with a narrow entrance between its eastern end and the outer wall. The alignment of these two entrances would seem to indicate that the fort's entrance, which has not survived, was somewhere on its eastern side, probably in the vicinity of the drop-shaped building.

Directions   (Time: 1 hour)

Take the Uig road (A856) from Portree and drive through Uig taking the road signposted to Kilmuir and Staffin (A855). After driving up the hill and negotiating the hairpin bend, continue on this road past the turning to the right signposted to the Quirang and Staffin. Just over a quarter of a mile later, you will pass a sign saying Kilmuir and then one advising of parking 450 yards ahead. About 200 yards past that second sign there is a farm road to the left. Although that track is passable in a car, it is very narrow and there is nowhere to park without obstructing farm vehicles. It is advisable to park your car in the parking area and then walk back along the road and go down the track on foot. The fort is visible on top of the hill on the skyline towards the coast. Follow the farm road down the hill and round to the left, until it turns right down to a house and farm buildings. At that point, fork left along the deeply rutted tractor track which runs beside the fields. As you approach the loch shore, you will see a gate on the right. Go through that gate and the one on the opposite side of the field. Cross the broken down stone wall and wire fence ahead of you and make your way up the hill to the fort by climbing diagonally to your right round to the NNE side of the hill, where a short scramble will bring you to the summit and the fort.

DUN LIATH (KILVAXTER)   (Map Ref: NG 360700)

Dun Liath is a pear-shaped fort, measuring 170 feet by 107 feet, with its pointed end to the north and its long axis running NNW to SSE. The north-western part of its wall, which runs along the edge of a cliff, has largely disappeared but was probably much lighter in construction, and possibly lower, than the walls in the other sectors, being only about 5 feet thick. The rest of the wall varies between 8 and 12 feet in thickness and, at the southern end, survives to a height of nearly 6 feet, although much of the interior face is obscured by fallen stones. Within the thickness of this wall are signs of at least two long galleries, one in the eastern part of the wall and one in the south, with entrances opening on to the interior of the fort. Entry to the fort was gained through a single, 3 feet wide entrance in the eastern wall, which is clearly visible, particularly from outside, with a well-preserved cell opening from its southern side, and a possible door check on the north. There is a hut circle, inside the fort, near to the end of the southern wall. Outside the fort, at its southern end, there is a double row of stones placed on edge, between a rocky outcrop at the end of the ridge on which the fort stands and the shore. These stones were presumably intended to impede any attackers approaching round the south-west side of the fort, and are thus similar in function to those noted at Dun Gerashader. About one and a half miles south-east of the fort, there is a small grassy mound, broken by a stone wall built across it, visible from the fort. This mound is the remains of Carn Liath (Map Ref NG 372688), the only square Hebridean chambered cairn on Skye, now much ruined.

Directions   (Time: 90 minutes)

From Uig take the A855 north to Kilmuir. About 6 miles north of Uig, turn left on to the minor road signposted to Bornaskitaig. Follow this road past where it turns sharp right and then for three quarters of a mile to a crossroads. Turn left at this crossroads and continue along this road to its end. You can park either beside the road or near to the slipway. Walk through the gate just before the sheep fank on the left and skirt round that structure, and then go through a second gate on to the hill. Head in a generally WSW direction over the ridge in front of you, skirting the rocky cliffs. Continue in that direction towards the coast, climbing over 2 or 3 ridges and crossing a couple of very marshy streams. The fort is not visible until you reach the summit of the penultimate ridge, when it appears as a tumble of fallen stones. Head towards the fort, aiming to approach it from the south and then climbing up the south-west side of the rise on which it stands, round the end of the walling.

DUN FLODIGARRY   (Map Ref: NG 464719)

Although this broch is fairly ruinous, it is one of the easier sites on Skye to reach and it provides a good excuse to visit the Flodigarry Hotel which, as well as being a very good place to have a drink or a meal, has connections with Flora MacDonald who lived for a time in a nearby cottage. The broch stands on top of a small rocky outcrop, behind the Hotel. The eastern segment of the walls has disappeared but the remainder of the walls still stand to about 2 or 3 feet. There is an entrance passage on the north west side and evidence of several galleries built into the space between the inner and outer walls.

Directions   (Time 15 minutes)

Take the Portree to Staffin road (A855) and follow it through Staffin and north along the coast. Continue past the junction with the road which turns off to the left towards Uig, and about two and a half miles north of that point you will see a signpost on the right to Dunans. About 200 yards further on, a minor road on the right is signposted to the Flodigarry Hotel. Drive down this minor road to the hotel and park in their car park. The broch is behind the Hotel in a walled garden. Since you are using the Hotel's private road and parking in their car park, it might be tactful to combine your visit to this broch with at least a drink in their bar, or a meal in their excellent Waterhorse Restaurant, although booking for the latter is advisable.

DUN SULEDALE   (Map Ref: NG 375526)

Dun Suledale is one of Skye's better preserved examples of a broch, although it is certainly not the easiest to reach. It is situated on top of a small rocky knoll in the middle of hilly, rough moorland which is often very marshy. The walls of the broch stand about seven feet high but the interior is filled with fallen stones and some fairly vigorous, and unfriendly, vegetation. There are signs of an outer enclosure wall around the broch. In the broch itself, there is a clearly defined entrance passage with a guard cell opening from its north side. Opposite this passage is a gallery built into the space between the inner and outer walls, which has the remains of a staircase at one end. There are also signs of other possible intra-mural galleries.

Directions   (Time: 90 minutes)

Follow the Portree to Dunvegan road (A850) for just under 7 miles, until it bends left away from Loch Snizort towards Loch Greshornish where, one mile beyond the road to Suledale (spelt Suladale on the OS map) village on the left, there is a track marked on the OS map leading south from the main road. Park your car on the remains of the old road which you will find on the right-hand side of the modern road, just past the start of that track. Cross the main road and walk through the gate and follow the track across the moorland for about a mile. The broch can be seen, albeit intermittently, to the left. There is no easy, or clearly defined, way to reach it. You have to cross some fairly deep and wide ditches and make your way across the very rough and boggy moorland. This is a monument which it is best to visit after a dry spell, but good waterproof boots are still advisable. Since the land around the broch is a grouse moor, your wandering across it during the shooting season might be both unwelcome and dangerous.

NORTH WEST REGION

DUN HALLIN

Dun Hallin is the best preserved of the three brochs which survive on the Waternish peninsula, and second only to Dun Beag on the rest of Skye. Its external walls stand to between 9 and 12 feet high on the northern side, showing clear evidence that the broch had been carefully constructed with large squared-off stones forming the lower courses. The outer wall has a distinct batter which would have given Dun Hallin the typical broch modern cooling tower shape. The entrance to the broch, which lies in the south-east quadrant where the external walls survive to little more than two or three courses, is visible although not well preserved, but there are no clear signs of galleries or intra-mural cells within the walls. Indeed, the whole of the interior is filled with fallen stones. Quite apart from its relatively well-preserved state, its commanding position on top of a natural rocky outcrop, around which there are traces of an enclosing wall, makes Dun Hallin an impressive monument which is well worth the small effort needed to reach it.

Directions   (Time: 1 hour)

Take the Portree to Dunvegan road (A850) and just outside Dunvegan turn right on to the B886 signposted to Stein and Geary. After 4 miles, turn right at the T junction up the hill towards the village of Hallin. Although Dun Hallin is clearly visible from this road, it is not quite as easy to reach as its position makes it appear. There are several ways to get to it, but all entail crossing some rough, and often very wet and marshy, moorland. From the map, the shortest route is from the Geary road but fences and some deep streams and ditches make the shortest neither the quickest nor the easiest route.

The best way to reach this broch is, after entering Hallin, to continue for just over half a mile. You will then see a long, low white bungalow on your left and a small tarmac track to the right with the numbers 16 and 17, indicating the numbers of the houses, on its corner. Drive up this track and park at the end. When I last visited Dun Hallin, the owner of the farm there urged me to continue in my car along a track which led past his farmyard and up the hill to the right, to save walking. All I will say is that his assessment of the cross-country capability of my car was more optimistic than my own and I felt obliged to decline, I hope courteously, his kind offer.

Having parked your car, continue on foot across the field in front of you, leaving the cottage on your right, to the gate which you will see ahead of you. Go through this gate, cross the stream and then, skirting the stream as it loops in front of you, follow the fence on your right up the hill. You will see Dun Hallin on the skyline ahead of you. Go through the small rusty gate in the right-hand corner of the field and continue up the hill to the broch.

DUN BORRAFIACH AND DUN GEARYMORE   (Map Refs: Borrafiach NG 235637
Gearymore NG 236649)

Although neither of these brochs is in a well preserved state, and Dun Gearymore hardly survives at all above the first two courses of its walls, the views across the Little Minch to the Outer Hebrides on one side, and the rugged moorland to the other, make the walk to them a memorable experience. The outer wall of Dun Borrafiach stands to nearly 9 feet at its highest point but is much lower near the entrance, which is in the north-west quadrant, and in the north-east quadrant. The internal arrangements are obscured by the fallen stones and other debris which fill the interior of the broch to a depth of 5 feet or more.

Dun Gearymore is even more ruinous than its neighbour with an outer wall which survives, for the most part, to scarcely more than two or three courses of stones. Like Borrafiach, its interior is filled with stones but signs of a gallery are still visible in the eastern part of the wall.

Directions   (Time: 2 hours)

From Hallin (see previous entry), continue north-west along the minor road to where it forks. The left fork is signposted to Trumpan; take the right-hand, unsignposted fork and follow this road for a further mile. At this point the road turns sharp left. Leave your car at this point and continue on foot through the gate, which you will see opposite the road down which you have just driven, and along the clearly defined track. Do not be tempted to take your car further since, although the track is easily passable for its first part, it quickly becomes deeply rutted and very muddy with nowhere to park or even turn a car round.

Despite the need to dodge the ruts and some of the muddier sections, the route to Dun Borrafiach and Dun Gearymore is an easy, pleasant walk with fine views of the Little Minch and the Outer Hebrides. Continue along this track for about one and a half miles. Just before you reach the ruins of Dun Borrafiach, you will see a pointed cairn on top of a hillock about 50 yards to your left. This cairn, which is most certainly not prehistoric in origin, commemorates a much more recent conflict than those which led to the building of the brochs. It is a restored memorial, with inscriptions in both English and Gaelic, to one Roderick MacLeod of Unish who was killed in the second battle of Waternish against the MacDonalds of Trotternish in about 1530. Continue along the track for a further four or five hundred yards and then strike off across the moorland towards Dun Borrafiach which is clearly visible up the hill to your right.

Dun Gearymore lies about threequarters of a mile north of Dun Borrafiach and can be reached by continuing along the track which led to Borrafiach and again striking off across the moorland to reach the remains of the broch some 150 yards to the right of the track. The remains of Dun Gearymore are clearly visible from the track but its ruinous state makes it more difficult to identify, at that range, as a broch rather than a mass of tumbled stones.

DUN FIADHAIRT
(Map Ref: NG 232504)

The inside of this broch was cleared some years ago but is now beginning to become very overgrown again. Despite this growth, the broch is much better preserved than its outside appearance would lead you to expect, with well constructed inner walls standing about 8 feet high. Dun Fiadhairt, although unusual in having two entrances, has most of the classic features of a broch. There are guard cells either side of the main entrance and a fine gallery which runs round the inside of the walls for about a third of their circumference. It is possible to walk round inside this gallery, albeit in a crouched position, but some of the overhead stones are becoming a little precarious and you should be careful not to dislodge them, both for the sake of the broch, and for your own safety. A staircase, of which six steps still exist, leads off a second gallery opposite, and to the left of, the entrance. The structure in the centre of the broch is the foundations of a later addition supplemented by fallen stones piled on top of it.

Almost directly opposite the main entrance is the second entrance which is about three feet high and pierces both the inner and outer walls of the large gallery. The purpose of this opening is obscure but it gives the appearance of being an original feature. The broch at Clickhimin, in Shetland, has two similar additional entrances, but these appear to give access to the roofs of outer defensive works. There are no signs of such outer defences at Dun Fiardhairt and the extra entrance there, if it is an original feature, seems to be a serious point of weakness in the broch's defences, without revealing any clear-cut purpose.

Directions
(Time: 1 hour)

Leave Dunvegan on the A850 towards Claigan. One and a half miles past the Dunvegan Castle car park and entrance, park your car in the space on the left of the road immediately after it crosses Loch Suarda. The route to the broch is easy to follow and is a very pleasant 20 minute walk, across relatively flat moorland with fine sea views. Climb over the gate, which is invariably locked, at the back of the parking space and walk up the track ahead of you. This track quickly deteriorates into little more than the ruts left by tractors but is still not difficult to follow for about half a mile until it reaches a narrow isthmus between two small bays. Dun Fiadhairt will have been visible ahead of you from the top of the hill before you descended to the isthmus. Cross the isthmus and continue up the track for two or three hundred yards before striking off right over the small rocky knoll, from the top of which you will again see the broch. The last bit of the walk to the broch tends to be a bit marshy in anything but the driest of weather. The easiest access to the broch is up a grassy path round the far side from where you approached and through the main entrance.

CLAIGAN SOUTERRAIN
(Map Ref: NG 238539)

Claigan Souterrain is smaller and less well preserved than the other examples on Skye but it is the easiest to reach. The interior is dark and usually very muddy; a torch is essential, and old clothes advisable, if you wish to do more than just peer through the entrance. The souterrain is a straight passage cut into the hillside, about three feet high and originally about 20 feet long. The first part of the passage has been destroyed and the present entrance lies about one-third along its original length. The partial collapse of the lintel over this entrance has considerably reduced its height making getting into it a matter of crawling on one's stomach (hence the earlier remarks about the need for old clothes). This low and narrow entrance opens into a stone-lined passage about three feet high and now about ten feet long, although it originally extended further into the hillside since its far end is blocked with mud and stones. Despite these changes, it is still a good example of this type of monument.

Directions   (Time: 45 minutes)

To reach the Claigan Souterrain, take the A850 out of Dunvegan, past where it crosses Loch Suarda and continue for one mile beyond the north end of the small loch, known as Loch Corlarach, on the left until you come to a T-junction. The left arm of the 'T' becomes a track leading to the Coral Beaches, while the right-hand arm heads towards Claigan. Turn left and park your car in the car park just before the Coral Beaches track and then walk up the right arm of the junction. After about 200 yards, the road turns sharp left; leave the road at this point and go through the gate which you will see ahead of you. Follow the clearly defined farm track up the hill, through a second gate until the track turns sharp right. The souterrain lies about 20 yards beyond this point, about 15 yards from the left-hand side of the track, but there is a large ditch with a heap of earth behind it which obscures the souterrain from the track and makes direct access difficult. It is easier if you continue along the track for a few yards, until the ditch narrows, before crossing it. Then walk back parallel to the track on the far side of the ditch until you come to the souterrain, which lies at the back of a small depression and is marked with a small metal plaque set in a low plinth. The walk to the souterrain is a gentle climb up a well-defined stony track, followed by no more than a few yards across moorland.

DUN OSDALE   (Map Ref: NG 241464)

Dun Osdale is a broch whose ruins stand in a commanding position on top of a small rocky hillock beside the Dunvegan-Glendale road. Although the walls are largely fallen, and the interior is blocked with tumbled stones, the double-walled circular form is clear and there are visible remains of some typical broch features. The entrance was probably on the east side of the broch, but there are only minimal signs of it remaining. There is a well-preserved oval cell within the walling on the west side and the entrance to a second cell on the south side. This second opening could have been the entrance to a gallery or a staircase but not enough survives to be certain.

Directions

The broch is on the left of the B884 Dunvegan to Glendale road, opposite a minor road leading to Uiginish, a turning marked by a board with a large wooden owl on top of it. Park beside the road and go through the gate and into the field. The broch is on your left on top of the rocky hillock. It is a fairly easy scramble to reach the broch.

DUN CHAICH
(Map Ref: NG 243477)

Dun Chaich is a small, oval-shaped fort standing on a knoll at the end of a rocky ridge which rises 20 to 30 feet above the surrounding countryside. This knoll is surrounded by sheer cliffs on three of its sides but, on its fourth, is joined to the ridge by a narrow neck of level ground. The fort measures 100 feet by 50 feet but most of the walling has disappeared, except at the south-eastern end where the foundation courses are still in place, and on the outer face of the south-western sector where sections of 2 or 3 courses are still visible. There is no clearly defined entrance, although what may be the left-hand side of a passage can be identified in the centre of the south-eastern wall which, from the geography of the fort, would appear to be the logical place for an entrance.

Directions
(Time: 30 minutes)

From the Dunvegan to Glendale road (B884), opposite Dun Osdale (see previous entry) turn right on to the minor road signposted to the Uiginish Hotel. Just over a mile after leaving the main road, the Uiginish road comes down to the loch shore. Opposite the small, low, rocky promontory on the seashore to the right, park beside the road and go through the gate on the left some 50 yards further down the road. Bear left up the hill in a WSW direction towards the rocky plateau which you will see ahead of you. Dun Chaich is at the extreme right-hand end of that plateau on a rocky pinnacle, joined to the rest of the plateau by a narrow neck of land. Dun Totaig (see next entry) is visible to the WNW, about half a mile away as the crow flies, but rather further as you walk.

DUN TOTAIG
(Map Ref: NG 238479)

Dun Totaig is a small, almost rectangular fort measuring about 75 feet by 40 feet, standing on top of a small rocky ridge. The remains of its massive wall can be seen on the north-west side standing to about 3 feet, with an entrance passage in the centre of the short side. There are signs of the ends of a cross wall just beyond where the entrance passage enters the interior of the dun, and a short passage built into the wall at the far end of the dun.

Directions
(Time: 40 minutes)

Leave the B884 Dunvegan to Glendale road opposite Dun Osdale, turning right on to the minor road signposted to Uiginish. Follow this minor road for about one and a half miles, past Dun Chaich (see previous entry) and park near the farm buildings which are just before Uiginish Lodge (now an hotel) at the end of the road. Walk up the track which leads off to the left, up the hill, through the gate and down to the right. The dun is on top of the small knoll on the right of the track just after the bend.

DUN BORERAIG   (Map Ref: NG 195532)

Dun Boreraig is set on a small mound on top of a cliff overlooking the north-east coast of the Duirinish peninsula. Although it is now much ruined, with its interior blocked by fallen stones and overgrown with vegetation, it has a number of interesting features which are still clearly visible. The top of the mound on which the broch stands was levelled and increased in size in antiquity by building up drystone retaining walls and filling the space between them and the original mound with earth. The resulting platform and its walls are still clearly visible, providing a flat area about six feet wide all round the outside walls of the broch with a larger platform, roughly triangular in shape, extending about 12 feet from the broch on its south-east side. There are signs of walling around the edge of this extended platform.

The outer wall of the broch remains to a maximum height of 9 feet on the south-east side but the inner wall is no more than five or six courses high. The lintels over the entrance passage on the NW side of the broch have collapsed but the passage itself is clearly defined with massive blocks marking its outer edge. There is a cell on the right-hand side of this passage but no visible connection between it and the passage itself. While this cell cannot be identified as a guard cell, it may have been similar in form to that at Dun Beag, where the cell next to the entrance opens into the broch interior rather than the passage itself, but may have fulfilled a similar function to guard cells elsewhere in providing a refuge from which defenders could attack anyone who managed to breach the entrance.

Directions   (Time: 50 minutes)

From the Dunvegan to Glendale road (B884) just beyond Colbost, turn right on to a minor road signposted to Galtrigill and Borreraig. Drive past the piping centre on the left and then park where a metalled track goes off to the right (there is just about enough room to park one car on the verge just before the track). You will see a conical monumental cairn on a headland in the distance to the right of the line of the road on which you were driving.

Having left your car, walk down the track and through the gate, turning immediately right and following the line of the drystone wall and wire fence which will then be on your right. The broch will appear on the skyline ahead of you on top of a rocky hillock and looking like a pile of tumbled rocks. It is much more impressive from the other side. Although there is no defined track to the broch it is generally easy walking, albeit with some marshy patches in wet weather.

DUN COLBOST

(Map Ref: NG 206495)

Although Dun Colbost is in a very ruinous state, a number of the typical broch features are still visible. How long they will remain so is questionable, since the broch is in danger of major collapse, unless it receives some considerable conservation effort in the very near future. In 1994, it had a notice on it warning of its dangerous condition; quite apart from being careful to avoid the risk of personal injury, it is important for visitors to the site not to do anything which could cause further damage to the broch itself. The broch is oval in shape, measuring 57 feet in diameter on a north-south axis, and 52 feet east to west, with walls about 12 feet in thickness. It occupies a strong defensive position on a plateau with steep, in places perpendicular, sides about 10 to 20 feet in height, which was reinforced by an outer defensive wall, roughly rectangular in shape, built close to the edges of the plateau. The entrance through this wall was probably in the north-west corner. The outer walls of the broch itself, built of large blocks of stone laid in courses, survive to a maximum height of 9 feet in the eastern sector, 7 feet in the north and 4 feet in the south but, in the western sector, little more than the foundation courses remain, and they are largely obscured by fallen stones. The interior of the broch is filled with fallen stones but the remains of a small gallery are visible in the eastern wall, which may well have given access to a staircase, although no steps survive today.   An entrance to a further gallery can also be seen in the northern quadrant of the inner wall. The position of the entrance to the broch cannot be determined but was, in all probability, located in the, now very ruined, western sector.

Directions

(Time: 1 hour)

Take the Dunvegan to Glendale road (B884) along the west side of Loch Dunvegan and through Colbost village. Just after passing through Colbost, the road climbs up a hill and then turns sharp left, where a minor road branches off to the right signposted to Borreraig. Immediately after the turn, there is a parking area on the left where you should leave your car. The Old School (now Skye Silver) can be seen across the valley to the right. Walk 100 yards further along the road and go through the small gate in the fence on the left. Bear right and head up the hill, passing above the electricity pole which you will see ahead of you. Continue up the hill, bearing left to pass between a rounded hillock and a rocky outcrop, to the top of the ridge, from where you will see the broch about 400 yards ahead of you on top of a rocky plateau. The broch is most easily reached by climbing the grassy slope on the north-west side of the plateau.

CENTRAL REGION

DUNAN AN AISILIDH   (Map Ref: NG 532357)

Dunan an Aisilidh is located near the end of a peninsula which curves round a bay on the east coast of Skye in the Narrows of Raasay. The dun is basically circular in plan with a diameter of 50 feet, but the northern sector of the wall curves inwards to follow the edge of the plateau on which it stands, making the dun roughly heart-shaped. In the north-east sector, the wall appears to have been extended in a north-westerly direction for about 20 feet along the top of a rocky peninsula. This extension was probably intended to prevent attackers using the peninsula as a base from which to assault the dun itself. Much of the walling has been reduced to little more than grassy mounds but, in the south-west sector, the outer face of the wall survives up to about 4 feet in height. The wall here is more substantial than elsewhere in the dun, measuring about 12 feet in thickness. Within this wall is a gallery, now filled with stones but its entrance, with its outer lintel still in position, is visible in the SSW sector of the inner wall of the dun. There are no signs of an entrance to the dun on its landward side but there is a possible entrance on the west side. Since the ground outside this entrance is less precipitous than elsewhere on the seaward sides of the dun, it may have been used as a watergate; certainly, the geography of the site makes it difficult today to reach this entrance by land from outside the dun.

Directions   (Time: 90 minutes)

Two miles south of Portree, turn off the A850 on to the B883, signposted to the Braes. After about 5 miles, fork left on to a minor road signposted to Balmeanach. Four hundred yards from this turn, there are two bungalows on the left, just beyond which is a parking area. Leave your car there and continue down the road for 300 yards to two white houses on the left with a small copse just beyond them. Turn off the road and walk between these two houses, cross the small stream by the culvert and then walk towards the sea keeping the wire fence on your right. Cross the isthmus and turn left towards the point. It is easier to walk along the summit of the ridge rather than closer to the shore, since the sides are crossed by numerous ditches. The dun is located on top of a rocky plateau just before the end of the point.

DUN DIARMAID   (Map Ref: NG 354382)

Dun Diarmaid is an oval dun measuring 51 feet by 47 feet which stands on a rocky knoll on the south shore of Loch Beag. On the seaward side, it is a strong defensive position rising steeply to 30 feet above sea level but it is easily approached from the land since the top of the knoll is only about 10 feet higher than its surroundings up a gentle slope. Very little is left of the walls, which were originally about 11 feet thick, but the lower courses of the inner face are still visible on the northern side and of the outer face in the south-west sector. There is no sign of the entrance but it was probably on the south side. Although this dun has largely disappeared, it is well worth the small effort needed to visit it.

Directions

(Time: 10 minutes)

Dun Diarmaid stands beside the Sligachan to Dunvegan road (A863) half a mile south of where it is joined by the road from Portree (B885). Park your car on the grass verge beside the road and then walk the twenty or so yards towards the sea to reach the dun which is clearly visible ahead of you.

DUN BEAG

(Map Ref: NG 339386)

Dun Beag is certainly the best preserved prehistoric monument on Skye and, unlike most of the other examples, considerable effort has been expended in clearing and maintaining it. It is easily accessible and clearly labelled with a plaque which gives a brief history of the broch and its use. There is even a designated car park for visitors to the site; such luxuries are, I fear, all too rare on the Island.

Although the Gaelic name, Dun Beag, may be translated as the Little Fort, this designation is probably to differentiate it from its much larger neighbour Dun Mor (the Large Fort) described below, rather than a comment on its size in general. In fact, Dun Beag is one of the larger brochs on Skye, with an external diameter of 62 feet and walls which vary from about 11 feet to nearly 14 feet in thickness. The outer walls of the broch survive in places to 11 feet in height and are built of large finished blocks. The entrance passage, on the east side, is broken down and the lintel stones which originally covered it have disappeared, although there are reports that they were still in place at the beginning of the last century. There are clearly defined checks for a door but no signs of holes for a bar to secure it.

On entering the broch, immediately to the right (north) of the entrance is a cell which opens on to the broch interior rather than in to the entrance passage, as is common with the guard cells in other brochs. While it is possible that this cell was similar in function to such guard cells, the very low entrance, which is only 2 feet 3 inches in height, would seem to limit its usefulness for that purpose.

To the left (south) of the broch entrance, there is an entrance to a gallery which, at one end, leads into a small domed cell and, at the other, to a staircase of which twenty steps survive. Opposite the entrance to this gallery, another entrance about 3 feet above the floor level of the broch opens into an intramural gallery which runs round over a quarter of the circumference of the walls. This gallery is about 50 feet long today but its ends are lost in debris, so that it may well have been even longer originally. The height of the entrance of this gallery above the floor of the broch, and the low entrance of the possible 'guard cell', could indicate that there was a verandah running round the inside wall at this level, presumably with a break at the broch entrance to give access to the interior.

Dun Beag was excavated by Countess Latour between 1914 and 1920, when finds dating from 100 AD through to the 18th century were unearthed. These finds, which are now in the Royal Museum of Scotland in Edinburgh, included a stone cup, a small quern, clay crucibles, a flat gold ring, two bronze buckles, an iron knife, an antler pick and an iron spear head. The stone objects probably date to around 100 AD, while the ring and buckles are probably Viking in origin. In additions coins were found dating from the reigns of Henry II, Edward I, James VI and George II and III. There was also evidence that the broch had been used for iron smelting at some period, probably well after its original occupation. It would appear that Dun Beag has had a long, and varied, history.

Directions   (Time: 40 minutes)

Follow the Sligachan to Dunvegan road (A863) through Struan. A minor road branches off to the left, signposted to Ullinish. Immediately after that junction, there is a small car park on the left. Park there, cross the road and walk through the small iron gate opposite. Continue up the hill for about 80 yards to the broch, which is clearly visible ahead of you. Although this is an easy walk, the ground can be a little marshy in places, particularly after wet weather. It will take no more than 10 minutes to walk up to the broch but it is worth taking time to examine it in some detail since it gives you an opportunity to see many of the typical broch features without the encumbrance of fallen masonry and vegetation, which so often obscure them in other examples on Skye.

DUN MOR   (Map Ref: NG 340390)

Dun Mor is situated on top of a rocky plateau which rises about 50 feet from the surrounding moorland. It is a natural defensive position with commanding views of the surrounding countryside and is protected on three sides by the almost sheer cliffs. The fort is rectangular in form measuring about 170 feet by 120 feet. It was originally enclosed by a wall but only the north-east section remains today. Even this section of wall is very ruined and, at first glance, appears to be merely a long line of tumbled stones. Closer inspection reveals the foundation blocks, and the remains of an entrance passage at the north end. The passage is about 6 feet wide, set in a wall which varies between 8 and 14 feet in thickness. There are also signs of an outer defensive wall, below the main one, on the east side of the fort.

Even though most of its walls have disappeared, enough remains to show that this fort was a very strong position which supplemented the advantages of its situation with strong defensive works. It is much less well preserved than its neighbouring broch at Dun Beag and more difficult to reach, but it is well worth the effort to have the chance to compare these two very different approaches to providing a stronghold for the community.

Directions

(Time: 1 hour)

From the broch at Dun Beag (see previous entry) walk due north across the moorland towards the steep rocky outcrop, which you will see ahead of you. Actually that walk is easier said than done, since the going is rough, criss-crossed by old dykes and ditches, and is very marshy in places. However, by carefully picking your way, you can avoid most of these hazards but good boots are probably advisable.

After about 600 yards or so, you will reach the foot of the outcrop on top of which Dun Mor is situated although you will not be able to see it at this stage. You can scramble up the south face, ie the one that is in front of you but, if that does not look particularly attractive, you can skirt round the foot of the plateau and approach the fort up the steep gradient on its north-east side (the direction which leads to the original entrance to the fort). Having reached the top of the plateau, you will find the remains of the main wall on the north-east side.

CNOC ULLINISH SOUTERRAIN

(Map Ref: NG 333385)

Although this souterrain is not particularly easy to find, it is well preserved and the walk to it is neither long nor difficult. It lies at the foot of a rocky cliff with the entrance in a shallow depression. The stone-lined passage, which is about 15 feet long and three feet square, slopes fairly steeply down from the entrance and then levels for the rest of its length. The far end of this passage is half-filled with mud and small stones but there is a small opening at the very end, which lies under a large stone slab set in the side of a further depression. It has been suggested that this depression could be the remains of a circular chamber which formed the end of the souterrain. While there are examples elsewhere which have such a chamber, there is insufficient remaining at Ullinish to be certain of its existence there.

Directions

(Time: 35 minutes)

The souterrain lies at the edge of a field off the minor road, opposite Dun Beag on the A863 Bracadale to Dunvegan road, which leads to Ullinish. It is probably best to park your car in the Dun Beag car park since the road to Ullinish is very narrow with few places where you could park safely. Walk down the Ullinish road for about half a mile until you reach a gate into the field on your right. There is a small sign at this gate pointing to the souterrain. Go through the gate and walk towards the rocky knoll which you will see ahead of you. At the foot of this knoll, bear right and walk round keeping the knoll on your left. After about 100 yards, the face of the knoll steepens and becomes a sheer rocky cliff. The entrance to the souterrain lies about 4 yards downhill from this rock face in a shallow depression in the ground. It was marked with a plaque set in a low plinth similar to that at Claigan but, in 1993, the plaque had disappeared leaving only the plinth. The far end of the passage, in a depression which may be the remains of a circular chamber, is about 5 yards further on, parallel to the cliff face. If you plan to go into the souterrain, old clothes are advisable since the height of the roof necessitates crawling and the floor is usually fairly muddy.

CNOC ULLINISH CHAMBERED CAIRN   (Map Ref: NG 324379)

Unlike most chambered cairns on Skye, Cnoc Ullinish has a clearly defined chamber while the cairn material, which would have originally covered it, has largely disappeared. This round Hebridean Group cairn would have been about 80 feet in diameter but little can be seen today of its material, apart from some grass covered mounds and lumps, although some of its perimeter can still be traced. The chamber measures 17 feet by 10 feet and consisted of large stones arranged in what Audrey Henshall describes as a "pear shape". Six of these stones remain standing to a height of about 2 feet, and there are signs of a seventh stump.

Directions

From the Sligachan to Dunvegan road (A863), after Struan, take the minor road, signposted to Ullinish, which branches off to the left opposite Dun Beag. About a quarter of a mile after this road bends sharp right at the Ullinish Lodge Hotel and heads NNW, the cairn can be seen in a field beside the left-hand side of the road. Access is by climbing over the fence but despite the presence of some plastic sheeting covering the top, barbed wire strand, some care is needed to avoid damaging the fence, tearing ones clothes or inflicting some fairly painful lacerations to one's person. Alternatively, the cairn can be viewed from the road.

TUNGADAL SOUTERRAIN AND HOUSE   (Map Ref: NG 408401)

While they are certainly not easy to reach, the souterrain and house at Tungadal are the best examples of prehistoric domestic buildings on the Island, and well worth the effort of getting there. The house, which probably dates from the Iron Age, has recently been restored by the Skye and Lochalsh Museum Service. It is about twenty feet long and its lower walls, consisting of a double layer of drystone walling with the gap between them filled with earth, stand about 4 feet high and would probably have been covered by a pitched thatch roof, supported by wooden posts. In form it would have probably looked like a smaller version of the old Skye black house, restored examples of which can be seen at various places around the Island. There is a stone hearth in the centre of the interior and an entrance passage at one end of the building.

The entrance to the souterrain is inside the house on the long side to the left of, and about 6 feet from, the entrance passage. This entrance opens into a passage about 3 feet square in size, which turns through 90 degrees to the right about 3 feet from the entrance, and then runs for about another 20 feet. There are openings in the roof above the turn and at the far end which provide light and ventilation but these are almost certainly not original features. While it is easy to enter the souterrain, provided you are prepared to crawl on your hands and knees, the floor is usually fairly wet and muddy, so old clothes are essential.

Directions

(Time: 3 hours)

From the Sligachan to Dunvegan road (A863), turn right at Bracadale on to the B885, Portree road and, immediately, turn right on to a minor road signposted to Totarder. After about threequarters of a mile, turn right across two bridges and then left and follow the road to its end. There is room to park at this point without obstructing either the road or the entrances to the house and adjacent buildings. Follow the clearly defined track to the right along the North side of Glen Bracadale with the river on your right. This part of the walk is easy with a clear, albeit deeply rutted in places, track and no more than gentle slopes for the first one and a half miles. However, do not be lulled into a false sense of security; things get more difficult later on.

After about one mile, and having passed a large farm building on the left, Loch Duagrich will come into view. Follow the track to the end of this loch and then turn right to reach the far side. Although the OS map marks a track running parallel with the end of the loch and then along the south shore, there is little sign of it on the ground. The best way is to follow the original track right to the loch end and then walk along the top of the bank which you will see there. It is tempting to cut the corner across the low lying ground near the loch but, be warned, it is extremely marshy and a classic example of speed and directness not being the same thing. At the end of the bank, pick your way towards the corner of the loch and then along its south side, keeping close to the shore. Any sign of a track at this point is rare. Towards the far end of the loch, you will come to a grass covered promontory; again a straight line may not be the quickest route and skirting the loch shore may be easier, and more comfortable, than ploughing through the near waist-high spear grass at this point.

Having got past this obstacle, the going becomes easier as long as you do not climb up the hillside where trenches cut for tree planting make walking difficult. Viewed from the end of the loch, the brow of the hill which forms the skyline on the right, descends steeply from right to left and then levels off into the flat moorland. At the bottom of this hill is a small grassy knoll about 150 yards from the end of the loch. The souterrain and house are on top of this knoll which, in 1993, was marked with a small wooden post.

As indicated, this is not the easiest of walks but it requires determination and reasonable weather rather than high levels of fitness. It also needs good waterproof boots and a certain amount of luck if you are not to get very wet feet when crossing the marshy ground at the end of the loch. On the credit side, you will, for the most part, be walking through some beautiful moorland scenery, with a most interesting prehistoric site at the end of it.

DUN FEORLIG

(Map Ref: NG 299424)

Dun Feorlig stands on a small promontory which extends out into the sea. It is circular in plan, with walls about 10 feet thick and 50 feet in diameter. Its dimensions are consistent with its having been a broch but insufficient of the walls remains to reveal any of the other broch features and it is therefore classified as a dun. Indeed the walls are little more than grassy mounds but the site is of interest since, to the north-west of the dun, there are the remains of what appears to be a defensive ditch, 3 feet deep and 10 feet wide, built across the neck of the promontory. Such ditch defences are rare on Skye, probably because of the difficulty of digging them in the rocky ground, and because of the ready availability of stones for walls.

Directions

(Time: 15 minutes)

From the Sligachan to Dunvegan road (A863), about four and a half miles beyond Struan, take the minor road which branches off to the left signposted to Feorlig and Harlosh. One mile from the main road, you will pass a field-gate on the left, opposite a house on the right. Park in the parking area beside the passing place on the left, about 100 yards past that gate. Walk back to the gate, go through it into the field and walk down towards the sea. The dun is clearly visible, slightly to your left, beyond the fence.

VATTEN CHAMBERED CAIRNS

(Map Refs: (North Cairn) NG 298441
(South Cairn) NG 299440)

Although the Vatten cairns have been somewhat battered by time, they are still substantial monuments which are well worth the small effort required to reach them. The North Cairn is about 90 feet in diameter and stands about 20 feet high today. It is built of relatively small rounded stones but some of the kerb stones around its perimeter are much more substantial, with some measuring over 3 feet by 6 feet, although others are considerably smaller. The South Cairn is about 100 yards from, and was originally rather larger than, its northern neighbour. Its diameter is between 110 and 120 feet but its height has been considerably reduced by robbing of its centre, which has left a deep depression. Despite this damage, the cairn is still some 11 feet in height. Although the depression in the centre of the cairn almost reaches ground level, there is no sign of a chamber or of the stones which formed it. After such extensive robbing, the absence of any sign of the chamber should not be taken as indicating that there was not one originally. Indeed, there are some indications that there was an entrance in the south-east face of the cairn.

Directions

(Time: 30 minutes)

Follow the Sligachan to Dunvegan road (A863) past Dun Beag and through Caroy. The cairns are visible on the side of the hill to the left of the road, immediately after the turn to the left signposted to Feorlig. There is a gate leading into the field in which the cairns are located, just after you have passed them, opposite a turning on the right signposted to Upper Feorlig.

DUN ARDTRECK (Map Ref: NG 335358)

Dun Ardtreck is a very good example of the type of promontory dun which it has been suggested should be known as a 'semi-broch'. There is a well preserved entrance, with checks for a door, and an upward sloping passage. The walls, which to the front remain to a height of about 8 feet, have galleries within them similar in construction to those in the brochs but there is no sign of any 'guard' cells at the entrance. The walls to the rear are little more than one course of stones in height; while they may have collapsed because of coastal erosion, it is unlikely that they were ever as substantial as those on the landward side, since the location of the semi-broch at the edge of a sheer cliff would hardly have necessitated very strong seaward defences. The interior is filled with fallen stones and over-grown with vegetation. There are signs of outer defensive works with an entrance some 50 feet east of the semi-broch.

Directions (Time: 1 hour)

From the Sligachan to Dunvegan road (A863) fork left at Drynoch on to the B8009. Follow this road along the shore of Loch Harport. At Portnalong, turn left towards Fiskavaig and, after half a mile, turn right on to a minor road signposted to Ardtreck. Follow this road for just under a mile until it bears left towards Fiskavaig Bay. Just before the metalled road finishes, by a gravelled parking area, a farm track forks off to the right at No 28 Portnalong (the number is on a very small sign, sunk in the grass of the verge). Walk down this farm track, through two gates and take the left fork aiming between the cottage and a white corrugated iron barn with a red roof, which you will see ahead of you. Just beyond these buildings is a fence which you should cross using the fairly rudimentary stile. Walk up the hill to the next fence, where you should turn right and walk beside the fence until you reach a gate. Go through the gate and climb the small rocky knoll ahead of you, from the top of which you will have a good view of Dun Ardtreck. Head across the moorland, keeping to the right-hand side of the small valley and then up the rise to the dun.

RUDH AN DUNAIN (Map Ref: (Cairn) NG 393164 (Dun) NG 396160)

Rudh an Dunain, although deserted today, is a particularly interesting site showing signs of habitation dating from the neolithic until recent times. The two main prehistoric sites are a chambered cairn and a well-preserved promontory dun, both situated near the shores of the small loch at the end of the peninsula. The wild beauty of this area, and the interest of its monuments, make it well worth the long and not always easy walk required to reach it.

The chambered cairn is a Hebridean Group, round cairn, about 65 feet in diameter, with a V-shaped facade, measuring about 24 feet across and 10 feet deep, in its western face. This facade originally consisted of large vertically placed stones with panels of dry stone walling between them. Most of these large stones have been displaced but there is a well preserved section of walling just south of the entrance. A narrow entrance passage in the middle of the facade leads into an ante-chamber. This passage is about 1 foot 8 inches wide and 2 feet 6 inches high, although the height at the entrance is now much lower because the first lintel has slipped outwards and downwards, making it a fairly tight, but practicable, squeeze to get in. It is a slightly sobering thought, as you ease your way into this chamber, that if any of the stones collapse and trap you, it could be a very long time indeed before anyone came to your rescue. The passage and the ante-chamber are together about 8 feet long, and lead into the circular central chamber which is about 7 feet in diameter, and now about 5 feet high. Originally this chamber, although now unroofed, would probably have had a few more courses of corbelling stones, closed with a single capstone, giving it a beehive shape. The exterior of the cairn is fairly ruinous but there are a few kerb stones still in place and three larger stones, one of which has fallen, marking the entrance. When this cairn was excavated in 1931 and 1932, finds included the remains of six adults and pieces of Beaker pottery.

The dun consists of a curved double wall made of rectangular stones now standing some 9 feet high at its centre. There are signs that, over the years, the cliffs on which this dun stands have been eroded, causing the ends of the main wall to collapse and the walls on the seaward sides to disappear altogether. The location of the dun on the edge of sheer cliffs probably means that the seaward defences were never as substantial as those on the land side, and may well have been only to guard against the occupants' falling off the edge. There is an entrance passage, checked for a door, at the western end of the wall and the remains of a gallery within the wall visible just east of the entrance and at the eastern end of the wall.

Directions   (Time: 4 hours)

The walk to Rudh an Dunain is some three and a half miles over rough paths which, since they cross a number of rivers and streams, only one of which is bridged, are best attempted after a dry spell. In anything but the driest weather, waterproof boots are advisable, particularly for the last mile or so which crosses some marshy moorland.

From the Sligachan to Dunvegan road (A863), turn left at Drynoch on to the B8009, Carbost road. One and a half miles later, turn sharp left on to the minor road to Glenbrittle. Park at the end of this road and then walk through the campsite to the toilet block at the far end. Cross the stile behind this block and follow the path which begins just below the water storage tank. The largest of the rivers, the Allt Coire Lagan, about one and a half miles from Glenbrittle, can usually be crossed using stepping stones but, if it is in spate, there is a bridge (which is not marked on the OS map) further up the hill to the right of the path, which requires only a short detour. The path divides later; you should follow the lower track which leads beneath the cliffs of Creag Mhor. The path becomes increasingly less well-defined but, by aiming between the shore and the slopes of Carn Mhor you will see a small loch ahead and slightly to your left. The chambered cairn is located in front of the wall beside the loch, and the dun can be reached by walking round the north shore of the loch and heading towards the coast. Although the edge of the loch is marshy, it is easier to stay close to the shoreline than to negotiate the very rough and bracken-covered land higher up.

DUN SLEADALE
(Map Ref: NG 324292)

This is not the easiest site to reach, since it involves walking nearly a mile across rough moorland while climbing over 500 feet. The broch stands at the end of a short rocky ridge in a high glen but, despite its elevation and being only half a mile from the coast, high ground to the west prevents any sight of the sea. In that respect, it is unlike most brochs on Skye. Although the broch is quite ruinous, in parts it is better preserved than many on Skye and some interesting features are still clearly visible. The outer walls survive up to 8 feet in the south-east sector, 5 feet in the east and north-east, but as little more than foundations in the south and south-west. The interior of the broch is full of fallen stones but there is a clearly defined, although again blocked with fallen stones, entrance in the east, with the unusual feature of a passage with slightly curved walls. Three feet in from the outer end of this passage there are checks for a door, that on the northern side being the better preserved. One of the passage's roof lintels is still in place. On the opposite (western) side of the broch is an entrance to a gallery, which may have run right round the north sector of the walls almost to the entrance passage. The broch is built at the southern end of a small platform which extends 25 feet beyond its northern side, which was protected on its northern side by, what appears to be, an earth and stone rampart.

Directions
(Time: 2 hours)

From the Sligachan to Dunvegan road (A863) at Drynoch, fork left on to the B8009 signposted to Carbost. Outside Merkadale, fork left again on to the minor road signposted to Talisker and Eynort. Follow this road past the Glen Eynort turn and down to its end near Talisker House. Park against the wall on the right of the road as instructed by the notice there, and then walk down the track, which runs beside Talisker House towards the beach. Go through the gate across the track and immediately turn sharp left up the hill, keeping the fence on your left. Follow this fence round to the left and then walk along the hillside parallel with Sleadale Burn on your left. It is advisable to work your way up the hillside since, eventually, you will have to cross over its ridge, and a slow traverse upwards is easier than a last minute stiff climb. After just under three quarters of a mile, the burn cascades down a series of stepped falls about 20 feet in height, into a pool. Just before you come abreast of these falls, strike right up the hill to the top of the ridge, aiming for the break in the rocky cliffs. After crossing two small streams and climbing up a fairly steep grassy slope to reach the top of the ridge, you will see the broch ahead of you. The easiest way to reach the broch is to approach it from the south-west.

ARD AN T'SABHAIL BROCH   (Map Ref: NG 318333)

Ard an T'Sabhail is a much ruined broch, some 56 feet in diameter with walls that are 9 to 12 feet thick, located in an excellent defensive position, the strength of which was enhanced by some fairly extensive outer defensive walls. The broch's condition has not been improved by someone piling up some of its stones to form a cairn on top of the remains of the northern sector of its walls. The best preserved section is in the south-east, where there is a clearly defined, although full of stones, entrance passage with a guard cell on its left-hand side. There are signs of a second cell on the other, northern, side but this does not appear to have connected with the entrance passage itself. There are also signs of a gallery within the northern sector of the walls. The broch interior is full of fallen stones but a scarcement, about 9 inches wide can be seen some 2 feet above these stones. The main outer defences occupy the rest of the plateau on which the broch stands, to the south-east of the broch. These consist of two roughly square courts, the outer of which is at a lower level than the inner, which extend 75 feet from the broch. The north-east walls of both courts have largely disappeared, but the course of the rest of the walling is clearly visible. There is a well-defined entrance at the southern end of the outer court but no sign of any parallel entrance into the inner. There are also signs of a wall running east from the north-east face of the broch to the edge of the plateau.

Directions   (Time: 1 hour)

From the Sligachan to Dunvegan road (A863), turn left on the Merkadale and Carbost road (B8009) just before Drynoch. About 6 miles from this turn, at Portnalong, turn left towards Fiskavaig. Three miles further on, after a sharp right-hand uphill hairpin bend, you will see to your left a rocky crag; the broch lies to the right of its summit at a slightly lower level. The pointed cairn built on its walls is clearly visible. Parking along this road is not easy but there is a small space next to the passing place on the left just before you reach the houses. Walk down the road and, just before the first house on the left, go through the gate and into the field to the left of the road. Walk up the hill and cross the fence at the other side of the field. Continue up the hill across the heather covered moorland. From the top of this ridge, you will again be able to see the rocky crag which you saw from the road. Head towards this crag and, at the base of its cliffs, turn left and skirt round to the far side where you will find a narrow break in the cliffs. Climb up the grassy, rock-covered slope which leads to the summit. At the top of this slope, you will see the remains of the broch ahead of you.

SOUTHERN REGION

LIVERAS CHAMBERED CAIRN
(Map Ref: NG 642238)

This Hebridean Group, round chambered cairn is now a grass covered mound, 13 feet in height, with trees growing out of it. It was originally about 77 feet in diameter but that diameter has been reduced by about 12 feet on the east side by the building of the road. A chamber, reported to measure 14 feet by 9 feet by 6 feet high, was discovered when it collapsed in 1832. This chamber was subsequently broken up and filled with earth but part of its capstone, measuring 8 feet by 5 feet by 1 foot thick, can be seen leaning against the north face of the cairn. A second, partially buried, smaller stone, measuring 3 feet 6 inches by 18 inches by 1 foot thick, is nearby. Finds include skulls and ashes, and wrist guards made of stone which are now in the National Museum.

Directions
(Time 10 minutes)

From the Sligachan to Broadford road (A850), turn left at the second turning on the left after you pass the sign saying Broadford, on to the minor road signposted to An Acarsaid. The cairn is on the left between two houses about 200 yards from the turning. It is probably easier to park in the parking area on the right of the main road, opposite the turning, and walk up the minor road to the cairn.

ACHADH A'CHUIRN CHAMBERED CAIRN
(Map Ref: NG 664235)

This monument is another example of a Hebridean Group round cairn, which is in an even more battered condition than its neighbour at Liveras, the other side of Broadford Bay. It is 80 feet in diameter but its height has been reduced to little more than 6 or 7 feet. On its NNE side is a stone, 5 feet long, lying on a south-east to north-west line, and a second smaller stone near the top of the cairn. It is not possible to say whether these stones were part of the chamber.

Directions
(Time: 20 minutes)

From the Broadford to Kyleakin road (A850), after leaving Broadford turn left on to minor road signposted to Waterloo. About 700 yards from the main road, there is a break between the houses on the right, opposite a small stone slipway on the left. Park your car by the side of the road and go through the gate on the right and walk towards the cairn, which appears as a grassy mound at the side of the field to the left of the one which you have just entered. Cross the fence by the cairn.

CLACH NA H'ANNAIT STANDING STONE   (Map Ref: NG 590203)

The single stone, which is about 7 feet in height, stands on a raised mound in the field next to the house at Kilbride. It is roughly square in cross-section with a slight bend in the middle. There are signs of old field enclosures and some possibly interesting bumps in the ground around the stone, but no real indications of any other stones or features. However, it is likely that this area was of importance in prehistoric times since a stone circle is thought to have existed on the far side of the house, although no sign of this monument remains today.

Directions   (Time: 20 minutes)

On the Broadford to Elgol road (A881), about 4 miles from Broadford, there is a sign on the right-hand side of the road, indicating left to Kilbride. Turn left here and follow the minor road for about 600 yards, to where a tarmac track on the right leads to a large white house and some farm buildings. Park your car by the road and walk down the track, turning right through a gate into a field just before you reach the entrance to the house's garden. Follow the stone wall round to your left and you will see Clach Na H'Annait standing on a slight mound ahead of you.

DUN RINGILL   (Map Ref: NG 562171)

Dun Ringill appears now to be a D-shaped semi-broch, although it is conceivable that it was built as a complete circular structure, part of which has since collapsed into the sea. Based on its present appearance, it is classified here as a semi-broch, similar to Dun Ardtreck but showing fewer of the features associated with the true brochs. If that classification is correct, Dun Ringill may well represent an intermediate stage in the development from the original form of promontory dun, typified by Dun Grugaig to the Ardtreck type D-shaped semi-broch. Such theories are always attractive, and may well have a great deal of logic behind them but, without firm dating of the various structures, they remain largely conjectural. Whatever its true place in the evolution of fortifications in Scotland, Dun Ringill is also interesting for its unusual entrance arrangements. The opening in the outside wall lies well below the level of the internal floor and the entrance passage consists of a sloping ramp which emerges near the centre of the enclosure. Perhaps this arrangement is similar in purpose to the barbican protecting the gate of a medieval castle but placed internally rather than outside the gate. It is almost certainly a later addition since it is built of different stone to the rest of the broch, showing that the structure was modified and re-used as a fortification after its initial use. There are also signs of later buildings both within the semi-broch and outside its walls.

Directions   (Time: 1 hour)

The route to Dun Ringill is a pleasant walk, first through mature woodland and then along a generally well defined coastal footpath. Only the last quarter of a mile requires walking across rougher ground. On the Broadford to Elgol road (A881) drive round the head of Loch Slapin and south for a further 4 miles to Kilmarie where, immediately south of the bridge over the river Abhainn Cille Mhaire, a minor road branches off to Kilmarie House. A quarter of a mile from the main road, walk through the gate in the fence just before the house and on the opposite side of the road to it. Follow the path, crossing the river by the bridge, down to the coast. Alternatively, you can cross the river using the stepping stones nearer the coast, but this route is not advisable when the river is in spate and, even in the best of conditions, requires a measure of agility and sure-footedness although, if you fail this test, you are unlikely to suffer anything worse than wet feet. Whichever route you choose, follow the coast walk beside the fence. When the you reach the corner of the field where the fence turns inland, cut the corner and continue along the coast until you come to a stile. Climb over the fence at this point and then follow the path on the landward side until the dun comes into sight. There is then a slightly less clearly defined path which leads down the hill and across the moorland to the dun.

CNOCAN NAN GOBHAR
(Map Ref: NG 553174)

This cairn is much ruined with much of its south-west side having been removed. It is also heavily overgrown with ferns and small trees which make discerning its outline very difficult. It is oval in shape with its long axis lying from NW to south-east and 72 feet in length. Despite the removal of large parts of the superstructure, no internal chamber has been found. In 1926, a beaker and some burnt human bones were discovered in a small cist near the top of the cairn.

Directions
(Time: 1 hour)

Follow the directions for reaching Dun Ringill (see previous entry) and from the field on the far side of the river from Kilmarie, opposite the stepping stones, climb over the two wooden stiles and skirt round the edge of the small wood. The cairn lies close to the north-east edge of this wood among a plantation of young (in 1992) trees. The area is crossed by numerous ditches dug as part of the tree planting programme which make the going a bit difficult. The walk from the stepping stones to the cairn and back will take about 20 minutes but boots are advisable as the ground is marshy in places.

NA CLACHAN BHREIGE STONE CIRCLE
(Map Ref: NG 543177)

Although there are only three of the stones still standing, Na Clachan Bhreige Stone Circle is the only example on Skye which is sufficiently complete to enable it to be positively identified as such. Even so, its original form is far from certain. Aubrey Burl suggests that it could have consisted of four stones only, in a roughly rectangular form, known as a "four-poster". On the other hand, if this monument was originally a true circle, it would, by extrapolation, probably have consisted of about ten or more stones and would have been some 90 feet in circumference. The existing three stones are about 9 feet apart and stand to 4 feet, 7 feet 4 inches and 6 feet in height respectively. The centre, and tallest of the three stones has tilted and is now inclined at an angle of about 30 degrees from the vertical.

Directions

(Time: 90 minutes)

Although the remains of this stone circle, on a heather covered mound, are clearly visible from the road, it is much more difficult to get to than you would expect. The problem is that the damming of the nearby river has resulted in the site becoming almost an island surrounded by some quite deep water and a mass of smaller ditches and some very marshy ground. Even in dry weather, you are going to need waterproof boots if you are not to end up with very wet feet indeed. On the Broadford to Elgol road (A881), a quarter of a mile south-west of Kilmarie, park your car in the parking area on the left-hand side of the road opposite the start of the footpath to Camasunary. Cross the stile and take this footpath until just before the narrow strip of woodland which intersects it at right angles. At this point, turn right across the moorland, circling round to the west to avoid the largest of the streams and ditches to reach the stones. There is no defined path and it is largely a matter of trial and error although having your objective always clearly visible ahead of you makes the navigation much easier.

ALLT NA CILLE SOUTERRAIN

(Map Ref: NG 53951417)

Allt na Cille is undoubtedly the most impressive, and the best preserved, souterrain on Skye; it is equally the most difficult to locate, taking my wife and I three visits before we found it, hence the 8 figure map reference for use on a 1:25,000 OS map. The passage is dug into a small knoll on the hillside. Its entrance is about 3 feet square but once inside it is possible to stand almost erect. The walls and floor are natural rock, although the floor is now covered with mud which has been washed into the souterrain, but the roof is formed of stone lintels about one foot in width. The passage was probably dug as a trench, the lintels placed in position and then covered with earth. The passage climbs at a shallow angle and then turns through 90 degrees to the right round a large rocky outcrop before continuing to climb for about another 15 feet tapering to about 2 feet square. There is an opening at the far end of the passage on to the top of the knoll, where it is marked by a ring of small stones but it is not clear if this back entrance, and its markings, are original features or later additions.

Directions

(Time: 90 minutes)

From the Broadford to Elgol road (A881), turn left on the minor road signposted to Drinan and turn right at the T-junction near the coast. Park beside the road just before it ends, but not in the turning place. Walk down the track, which continues beyond the end of the road, to a gate just before which you will see a ring of stones, feet in diameter about 50 yards to the left of the track. These are the remains of Dun Liath, Elgol, a dun. Continue through the gate, past the modern house on the left and down into the wooded valley. Cross the stream and continue along the track up the hill on the far side for about 50 yards, until the slope on the right-hand side becomes less precipitous. At that point strike off at right angles to the track up the hillside to the right. Where the land levels off, you will see the ruins of a building among signs of former cultivation. Behind these is an old stone dyke and two birch copses. Go between these two copses and cross the dyke. Turn slightly left and head up the hill to the top of a rounded knoll which you will see ahead of you, with a conical stone about 2 feet high on its front edge. The rear entrance to the souterrain is close to that stone and is marked by a ring of stones set in the peat. The front entrance, the one to be used to get into the souterrain, is cut into the side of the knoll facing the modern house which you passed earlier on the other side of the valley. As a check on your position, the knoll and its souterrain are almost due west of the house and half way up the higher ground beyond the birch copses.

DUN GRUGAIG (Map Ref: NG 535123)

Dun Grugaig is an impressive promontory fort with particularly massive walls on the landward side. There are no signs of walls on the seaward sides and, while the steep cliffs make such defences unnecessary there would, presumably, have been some form of light wall to stop the occupants falling to their doom. This risk certainly exists today, so you should note the warning at the end of the directions below. The landward wall is about 15 feet thick and stands to a height of 12 feet at its southern end. There is an entrance passage in the centre, 3 feet wide and 4 feet high at the entrance but increasing to 5 feet high at the inner end of the passage. Although the inner lintel has fallen, the passage roof remains intact for 12 feet of its length. The outer lintel is a massive stone block, trapezial in shape with its base being 5 feet 6 inches and its top 3 feet in length while its height is 2 feet. The ends of this wall, and any walling on the seaward sides of the fort, have been lost, probably by coastal erosion.

Directions (Time: 30 minutes)

From Broadford, follow the A881 to Elgol. At Elgol, before the road goes down a steep hill towards the jetty, turn left along a minor road, signposted to Glasnakille, which crosses to other side of the Strathaird peninsula. At Glasnakille, turn right for half a mile. Soon after the road winds down into a small valley and up the other side, you will see a white cottage on the right and both sides of the road are fenced. Park your car on the verge and facing the fence on the left-hand side, turn to your left and walk back along the road to where, at a stile, the fence turns down towards the coast. Do not cross the stile but scramble down the steep slope through the wood, keeping the fence on your right until the stile at the bottom corner. Continue straight ahead through the small clump of silver birch trees and out on to the point, where Dun Grugaig lies at the top of the cliff. Care is needed while exploring this dun since the cliffs on which it stands are high and the edges unguarded and, in some places, hidden by the vegetation. This no place for young children or excitable dogs.

BIBLIOGRAPHY

Burl, A., **The Stone Circles of the British Isles**, Yale University Press 1976.

Callander, J. G., 'Report on the Excavation of Dun Beag, a Broch near Struan, Skye.' **Proceedings of the Society of Antiquaries of Scotland** 40 (1920-1) 110-131.

Dyer, J., **Ancient Britain**, London 1988.

Feachem, R., **A Guide to Prehistoric Scotland**, London 1977.

Henshall, A. S., **The Chambered Tombs of Scotland**, Edinburgh 1963 and 1972.

MacKie, E. W., **Scotland: An Archaeological Guide**, London 1975.

MacSween, A., 'The Brochs, Duns and Enclosures of Skye.' **Northern Archaeology** Vols 5 and 6 (1984-5).

Megaw, J. V. S. and Simpson, D. D. A. (eds), **Introduction to British Prehistory**, Leicester and London 1979.

Ritchie, G. and A., **Scotland: Archaeology and Early History**, London 1981.

Ritchie, G. and Harman, M., **Exploring Scotland's Heritage: Argyll and the Western Isles**, Edinburgh 1985.

Ritchie, J. N. G., **Brochs of Scotland**, Princes Risborough 1988.

Royal Commission on the Ancient and Historic Monuments of Scotland, **Inventory of Ancient and Historical Constructions in the Outer Hebrides, Skye and the Small Isles**, Edinburgh 1928.

INDEX